B. Conscious Enterprises Presents:

# THE
# DIARY OF A BLACK MAN

BY: TONY B. CONSCIOUS
© 1998 B. CONSCIOUS ENTERPRISES

## "DIARY OF A BLACK MAN"
### copyright © 1998 B. CONSCIOUS ENTERPRISES
### FOR CONSCIOUS PUBLICATIONS™
### 1ST EDITION...

ALL RIGHTS RESERVED.
NO PART(S) OF THIS BOOK
OR TITLE MAY BE REPRODUCED
OR UTILIZED IN ANY SHAPE
OR FORM WITHOUT WRITTEN PERMISSION FROM THE
PUBLISHER

Cover Art by Nic The Artist

*THIS BOOK IS DEDICATED TO:*

# RONALD YAO MARSHALL
### (JUNE 17, 1948 - SEPTEMBER 20, 1998)

*The ONLY person who has ever said to me:*

# "I'M PROUD OF YOU...
# JUST KEEP ON DOIN' WHAT YOU'RE DOIN'...
# DON'T LET NOBODY TELL YOU NOTHIN' ELSE..."

## ACKNOWLEDGEMENTS

I, TONY B. CONSCIOUS, as the author of this book, would like to acknowledge all of the African spirits and souls lost in the middle passage, African Diaspora and the African Holocaust which is still going on to this day.

I also would like to acknowledge the Creator, all of the Ancestors' spirits, my queen mother, my father and my soul mate, BEST FRIEND and spiritual guide... QUEEN SISTAH CHARMAIN. Without any one and/or all of the above mentioned, this book nor I would even be in existence.

Lastly, I would like to acknowledge all of the REVOLUTIONARY African poets, activists, writers, scholars, teachers, musicians, singers, actors, inventors, doctors, lawyers, everyday blue-collar workers and all those unemployed who year after year, decade after decade continue to fight to free African people's minds, bodies and spirits from the hells of North America, Europe and all of its colonies worldwide.

## *MAY THE STRUGGLE CONTINUE!!!*

# DIARY OF A BLACK MAN

| | |
|---|---:|
| INTRODUCTION | 7 |
| DIARY OF A BLACK MAN | 9 |
| 2B | 12 |
| GROWING | 14 |
| LATIN CONNECTION | 16 |
| HALF-BRED | 18 |
| IT AIN'T OVER | 20 |
| THE TREE | 23 |
| EYES | 24 |
| HOW BLAK? | 26 |
| FLOWER | 28 |
| THIS STRANGE LAND | 30 |
| IF I MUST DIE | 32 |
| SISTAH, SISTAH | 34 |
| DAMN!!! | 36 |
| L.A. | 39 |
| SMOKED | 42 |
| GONE WITH THE WIND | 44 |
| STRUGGLE | 46 |
| THE DREAM | 48 |
| WHERE IS MY QUEEN ? | 50 |
| RAIN | 53 |
| "FUCKED" | 55 |
| CAN WE LOVE? | 57 |
| BITCH | 58 |
| FREE | 60 |
| ZOO | 62 |
| SLAVE SONG | 64 |
| NFL | 66 |
| PART | 68 |
| LOOK | 70 |
| TIES | 72 |
| NEW SHOES | 74 |
| DARK SHADOWS | 76 |
| MY SOUL | 77 |
| RELAXED | 79 |
| DO OR DIE | 81 |
| PROGRESS | 83 |
| WORDS | 85 |
| O.J. | 88 |

DIARY OF A BLACK MAN....

| | |
|---|---|
| SOURCE | 90 |
| WHATDOUWANTWITHMYSISTAH? | 92 |
| GUN CONTROL | 95 |
| BROTHA 2 BROTHA | 98 |
| HYPOCRITE OR RADICAL ? | 101 |
| SEXPERIENCE | 103 |
| BOTTLE OF WINE | 106 |
| WATCH | 108 |
| FAREWELL | 110 |
| THE SOUL THAT NEVER WAS | 112 |
| DEATH BED | 115 |
| RIGHT ABOUT NOW | 117 |
| VOICE | 120 |
| LOVED TO DEATH | 122 |
| WHEN? | 124 |
| HOLLYWOOD | 126 |
| B-CONSCIOUS | 127 |
| OF | 127 |
| D-KNOWLEDGE | 127 |
| JUICED | 129 |
| ABORTED | 131 |
| DYING | 133 |
| A "G" THANG | 135 |
| SLAVE THREADS | 137 |
| SOMETHING | 139 |
| ESCAPE | 141 |
| LAZINESS | 143 |
| BROTHERHOOD | 145 |
| THE ARENA | 147 |
| NOTEBOOKS | 149 |
| PENNIES FROM HEAVEN | 151 |
| TRICKERY | 152 |
| LATINO RELATIONS | 154 |
| HIP-HOP | 156 |
| DESIRE | 158 |
| ABOUT THE AUTHOR: | 160 |

# INTRODUCTION

Have you ever read **THE DIARY OF A BLACK MAN?** A book or pad full of heart-felt feelings in which a tremendous amount of **GROWING** is taking place? Well, for those of African descent in America, whether they are considered **HALF-BREEDS** or have a **LATIN CONNECTION** in their bloodline, the task of self-identification is a laborious one and even for me, **IT AIN'T OVER**. Most of us cannot go back to **THE TREE** of our family's history nor do many have the **EYES** to see just **HOW BLAK** we really are.

Just like an exotic **FLOWER** replanted in **THIS STRANGE LAND**, I know IF I **MUST DIE**, I want to die an African. So, **SISTAH** my **SISTAH** and **BROTHA 2 BROTHA,** I say it's a **DAMN** shame how in cities like **L.A.** our people are all **SMOKED** out while most of our dreams are completely **GONE WITH THE WIND**. As I mentioned earlier, the **STRUGGLE** continues to fulfill **THE DREAM** of the slave, as so many brothas ask themselves **"WHERE IS MY QUEEN?"**. Many find that walking in the **RAIN** helps them cope with the **FUCKED** situation America has us in, But, **CAN WE LOVE** ourselves to the fullest even though life is a **BITCH** and we're not truly **FREE** ? The animals in the **ZOO** feel what we feel too, as we still sing our **SLAVE SONGS** and they beg and plead **2B** returned to their original homes also.

Another important issue is the fact that too many of our people are caught up in sports like the **N.F.L** and don't use the **PART** of their brains that make them look like the geniuses that they are. All of that **TIES** into the media who would much rather see us stealing **NEW SHOES** than dealing with our **DARK SHADOWS** that exclaim how much our souls wish they could just be **RELAXED**. It's a mission of **DO OR DIE** as we try to make **PROGRESS** but just get our words ignored by a group of people who'd much rather focus on **O.J.** than the **SOURCE** that made him what he is. This is why we should ask all the Caucasians **"WHAT DO YOU WANT WITH MY SISTAH?"** For, now they use **GUN CONTROL** to keep us from talking **BROTHA 2 BROTHA,** uniting and becoming conscious, militant revolutionaries.

You need to ask yourself "Is it the **HYPOCRITE OR RADICAL** one should follow?" For, in the 90's, even our **SEXPERIENCES** after having **A BOTTLE OF WINE** are quite western in their ways. If you think I'm lying, go to a African-American movie and just **WATCH** as we say **FAREWELL** to traditional African mating rituals and Hell-low to the styles of he who possess **THE SOUL THAT NEVER WAS**.

Even on the **DEATH-BED**, our people are praying to the wrong God **RIGHT ABOUT NOW**. Is it that we don't hear the Creator's **VOICE** in our heads or that Jesus was meant to be **LOVED TO DEATH** ?

When will we stop thinking **HOLLYWOOD** is going to **B-CONSCIOUS OF D-KNOWLEDGE** out there ? How many times must we get **JUICED** before we realize that everything in this system is designed to make sure our African intuition, ideas and concepts get **ABORTED** at the time of conception ? What makes it even worse is the fact that while our spirits are **DYING**, they fill our children's heads with all of these fantasies about life being **A "G' THING.**

If we could just take off those damn **SLAVE THREADS** and make **SOMETHING** of ourselves, we might escape the consumer madness that, due to **LAZINESS**, keeps our people in financial jeopardy.

**BROTHAHOOD** and fighting Uncle Sam in the **ARENA** are the only ways we as a people are going to do anything other than fill NOTEBOOKS with **PENNIES FROM HEAVEN** that we hope will make us dollars from the industry. They continue to use their **TRICKERY** and our unstable **LATINO RELATIONS** to keep us down. That's why, just as sure as our people will be creating and inventing **HIP-HOP**, the **DESIRE** will be in brothas like me to make sure that our poetry represents the true feelings and virtues of the masses of **BLACK** men in Amerikkka. Hopefully, this book will be a learning, growing and entertaining experience for you and afterwards.... I'll be able to read YOUR "diary" also.

Much love, peace and light.

## TONY B. CONSCIOUS

DIARY OF A BLACK MAN....

# DIARY OF A BLACK MAN

Born I was, in a hospital bed

Not in the infirmary, but the waiting room instead

Eyes partially open, I came into this world

Not in the arms of a nurse, but a teenage black girl

No money, no insurance, no immediate father

"DAMN !" exclaimed my mother, "I wanted a daughter"

Immediately catapulted into unfamiliar surroundings

The ghetto... that's where I'd receive my groundings

The filth , the stench, the jungle, I learned to call home

The rats, the roaches, the fleas, I learned to call my own

Watching a mother struggle, unprepared at 17

With one pair of flats, one pair of heels , one dress and a pair of jeans

No diploma, no G.E.D, only knowledge of herself

Strugglin', workin' hard, knowing there was no one else

To school I went, and with friends I grew

Learning only what society wanted me to

BLACK: EVIL, BAD.....WHITE: ANGELIC, GOOD

DIARY OF A BLACK MAN....

Police and politicians made sure this was understood

There was no escape from the system's traps

College wasn't an option, only the army, hustlin' or sellin' crack

So hustle I did, both night and day

Especially when mom insinuated another was on the way

Loser after loser vacationed in her life

But none was man enough to make her a wife

So, man of the house I was, with street knowledge in my head

Nickel and dimin', petty crimin', I kept my family fed

Momma worked to jobs and at both "whitey" harassed her

Tried to sex her, disrespect her and called me a bastard

Making me see the world through smoke filled glasses

The oppressed versus the oppressor, "Uncle Sam" versus the masses

The white man, self righteous, ENEMY OF ALL

Controlling and coercing behind his social walls

I remember my adolescence well, now that I've come to light

After an extensive search for guidance

A deep evaluation of my plight

A painful journey through the effects and the cause

The reactions, trials and errors, plus God-made laws

DIARY OF A BLACK MAN....

The concepts and reconstruction that both made me strong

A fighter, a revolutionary, a bird with a song

A man who's thoughts will live forever, because he had a plan

A dream, a destiny, a diary... of being a black man

# 2B

2B or not 2B... this is the question...

2B a man and tell the world how I REALLY feel
Or
2B afraid of backlashes and the chance of being killed
2B strong and stand up, even rebel if I must
Or
2B weak and just go along, all the time feeling disgust

2B or not 2B... this is the question...

Shall I B that African warrior, inventor and creator ?
Or
Shall I B that American Negro, that Uncle Tom, that self-hater ?
Shall I be concerned with the children and their pain ?
Or
Shall I only be concerned with monetary gain ?

2B or not 2B...this is the question...

Shall I B that European-lovin', joining the army, fool ?
Or
Shall I B the liberator of African minds, by opening my own school ?
Shall I go along with plots to defamate my leaders ?
Or
Shall I say REVOLUTION and get my nine millimeter ?

2B or not 2B...this truly B the question...

Shall I give up and give in, believing things won't ever change ?
Or
Shall I study my ancestors ways and vow 2 B the same ?
Shall I do what others do everyday to fit in and be cool ?

DIARY OF A BLACK MAN....

*Or*
*Shall I do what I know is right, knowing I'll B ridiculed?*

*2B or not 2B...*

**WHAT IT REALLY COMES DOWN TO IS:**

*Shall I B meek, timid and ignore other's sins*
*Or*
*Shall I still B-Conscious and B the fighter, that I've always been?*

DIARY OF A BLACK MAN....

Back
Back
I go
From which I came
Wishing all my peoples' would do the same
A renaissance, does it hold the key, the keys ?
Tell me what today this new so-called "Negro" sees
I watch children act as if our ancestors
Never existed or perhaps lived better
If "Jesus" was nailed to the cross
Paid the cost and all sin was lost
Then tell me why am I still
Invisible
Like Ralph Ellison's
"Invisible Man"
I am
I am
Unseen, unheard
And my words
Fall upon deaf ears I fear
This new generation of Blak people
Were taught by the last full of Blak evil
Scared to stand up, scared to lose,
So sleepy they slept and now their children snooze
Thinking being a gangstah is a position of prestige
Unconsciousness and ignorance this will breed

DIARY OF A BLACK MAN....

*Needs reevaluation, this Blak nation*

    *Faces annihilation, Due to alienation*

      *From the youth, hidden from the truth*

    *As I search for secrets and clues like a sleuth*

   Who am I ?  What am I ?   Do I know ?

In pain,  I search,   I wonder,  I learn,   I hurt,

# *I grow*

DIARY OF A BLACK MAN....

# LATIN CONNECTION

I say "Que Pasa ? whaddup whaddup waddup ?
Tienes Dinero ?" as I hold out my cup
But nobody hears me as I walk through the barrio
Nobody hears me in the hood, they all say "sorry bro"
I say "Como se llama, muchachita ?" or "What's your name?"
"You're a beautiful young girl" I say, cause I got game
"Me llamo Tony or B-Conscious ya know ?"
"Do you have a boyfriend ?" or "Tienes Nabio ?"

But does she hear me though ? I really can't tell
I say "Adios senorita," DAMN, oh well
A muy bonita senorita is really hard to find
Esa's and cholo's be like"Say bro...why don't you stay with your own kind"
I say "Well that's fine, but tell me why time after time..."
"I see your women with WHITE men, even more than I see mine"
"And hold up, why are you so friendly to the white man ?"
"I'm MORE your friend and you don't even speak to me, I DON'T UNDERSTAND"

"Is it that the LATINO or SPANISH has made you forget..."
"That the so-called Latinos are really INDIANS,
And the WHITE MAN stole your shit !!!"
"And the fact that Indians and Africans used to trade goods before THEY came"
"Matter of fact, INDIANS ARE AFRICAN, so we're one in the same !!!"
"Oh but you forgot that, you don't remember the solution..."
"GERONIMO, SITTING BULL and CAESAR CHAVEZ told you...REVOLUTION"
"Know me not, but if you're scared, admit it..."

DIARY OF A BLACK MAN....

*"I'm scared too, But at least I'm committed !"*

*"Oppressed in the same slums, smelling the same stank"*
*"Same welfare card we have, same Food Bank"*
*"Same system, same fascist, who stole us from our land..."*
*"Raped and killed you ancestors too, and shackles your bronze hands."*
*"So together and ONLY TOGETHER, we shall live on"*
*"The environment, the people, LA RAZA, if we bond"*
*"We've both tried alone through protest, peace and election..."*
*"Ain't you tired yet ? Now you're seein' the LATIN CONNECTION !!!"*

# HALF-BRED

Let me tell you a little story about a kid I know
Just like you and me, but did he see like we?  Oh no
He was black, but a fact only by the rule
One-eighth with self-hate that he learned in school
High-yellow with a streak, a shade, a stream
A little color in the stream, but still mainstream
Too mulatto, school model, grew up to confused
Too macho and like the lotto, didn't really want to lose
So unite?  not quite, cause he could really fit in
With the WHITE man, so understand, only like a tan was his skin
Couldn't deal with the BLACK side, the pride, so leave him alone
Didn't know what to do with a white pops at home
Does he learn?  Does he burn?  Give up everything he's had ?
Or disrespect and neglect, like moms got from dad ?
This is what happens, it happened and is still happening everyday
To mixed children, we keep building by mating this way
Not to say it's not O.K., alright or even wrong

I'm just trying to hip ya and equip ya to go on
Blacks got enough trouble and we huddle to get it right
Unite we try, but it's much harder for half-whites
Neglected, TOO LIGHT, TOO DARK is the shade
Either side of the coin equals the same fade
Somebody got faded...and faded is their dilemma
And for the HALF-BREED indeed, the light is much dimmer....

# IT AIN'T OVER

From the depths of the dark continent we were nabbed

Fighting , kicking and yelling as we were grabbed

Running , pulling away, even committing suicide

Begging, pleading, and trying to hide

"LEAVE US ALONE !!!  PLEASE LET US BE !!!"

"Why must you try to enslave the free ?"

Sly you slithered and struck like a cobra

But Africans said "IT AIN 'T OVER !!!"


Packed like sardines, on ships cold and dark

Rather than submit, we'd  jump to the sharks

To the new world we came, instantly receiving whip marks on our shoulders

Under our breaths exclaiming: "    IT AIN 'T OVER !!!"


Nat Turner with disgruntled souls, sent a message to you

Sam Sharpe followed, as did Marcus Garvey too

Harriet Tubman's "underground"  helped many of us escape

The beatings, the lynchings, the shootings and the rapes

To the north we went bruised, blak, and poor

To stamp out slavery, we fought in a Civil War

Thinking it was over, but America got colder

As you in turn said to us, "IT AIN 'T OVER !!!"


Days, weeks, months and years would pass

As we dealt with our position:   2nd CLASS


DIARY OF A BLACK MAN....

Slowly but surely getting energy to stand and fight

Then in what seemed like overnight..... TA-DOW---- CIVIL RIGHTS !!!

Martin tried, you killed him. Malcolm tried also

The Blak Panthers came to the rescue, and ....well, you know

You wanted to see us passive, and drunk instead of sober

But under our breaths, Blaks still muttered : "IT AIN 'T OVER"

So through the 70's we went, awaiting with open eyes

Preparing, sharing , growing and taking notes for our next rise

As you searched, raked, shuffled and put laws into play

Cut programs and did EVERYTHING to take back the progress made

The 80's came and a new system using drugs and booze

Gang bangin' and genocide you inspired, filled the daily news

A man made virus called A.I.D.S was your "ace in the hole"

You said " They're getting stronger and more educated, FUCK IT !

We'll kill 'em all to keep control"

Decrease the population, make us kill our own

From Baghdad to Somalia, and in ghettos here at home

We thought you were done with your evil deeds

But just like a dog named Rover

You can't teach an old dog new tricks, so we knew it wasn't over...


Your constant oppression, brainwashing of our minds

Stealing our culture, killing our people, while "Uncle Tom" kisses your behind

Your contradictions, half-truths and lately glorification

Of police and government urban confrontations

Annihilation ? In situations with sophistication

You justify your ANTI-BLAK, Anti- ethnic retaliation

DIARY OF A BLACK MAN....

I know you think you can stop us, but I hope you have a clover
'Cause we were the first to come and we'll be the last to leave, so be prepared...

                    IT AIN'T OVER !!!

DIARY OF A BLACK MAN....

# THE TREE

From the dirt of God's earth comes roots
Growing bigger and bigger with time
Erupting from down under, reaching for the heavens
Peering anxiously at the skyline
Forever inching their way towards the clouds

Retaining history memory and reason
Branching out, sprouting, getting stronger and longer
Growing and learning through the seasons
WE ARE THE TREES, with roots long and deep

Going far into the ground beneath us
Intertwined they are, knotted and leading
To the grave sites of ancestors who had to leave us
Leaves growing, changing; green , maple brown

As we stay, we sway in the wind
Growing older, our trunks which signify knowledge
Thicken like layers of skin
At one with nature, universal in form

We relate openly to the birds
To the insect, the dog, the cat, the mammal,
The bear, the snake, and the squirrel
Tell me, why must people take our knowledge

Cut it and build a civilization with our trunks ?
Warm themselves by burning us
Leaving our roots discarded and in chunks
so many try to deny our importance

For they don't TRULY see
As long as there's nature, seasons and god
There will always be The TREE...

# EYES

*When I look into someone's eyes, sometimes I see*
*Beyond the outer person, into the mystery*
*The soul, the essence, the being, the deepest darkest part*
*The nature of an individual, the innocence, the heart*

*When I look into LIGHT eyes, I used to often stare*
*And wonder what I saw and why I saw it there*
*After years of being bewildered, I now know why*
*I see what I see and feel what I feel, when I look into someone's eyes*

*When I look into BLUE eyes, I see the seas*
*The oceans wide and dark, the waters cold and deep*
*I think of slave ships rolling, a captain and a crew*
*With my ancestors who were packed like cargo, trying to make it through*
*I think of all the ones who died, when I see eyes of BLUE*
*I think of the Atlantic and Pacific, which they often went into*
*I see the skies and I see the Creator, somewhere up above*
*And I wonder why my people suffer, and if it's out of love*
*I see the BLUE that's in the "American Flag" and the freedom once sought*
*That same freedom my people fought for and died for, but never, ever got*

*Now when I look into GREEN eyes, I first think of leaves*
*Grass, plants and animals, then I think of trees*
*Trees on which my ancestors hung, because there had to be*
*People GREEN with envy, hate and bigotry*
*GREEN eyes to me, what do they symbolize ?*
*Dead presidents who once owned slaves on GREEN dollar bills*
*DAMN THEM GREEN EYES !!!*

*Now when I look into BROWN eyes, LIGHT BROWN, let me explain*
*I see the sands of Egypt and fields of golden grain*
*When I see DARK BROWN EYES, I think of Egypt again*

DIARY OF A BLACK MAN....

*But I also think of Kenya and Ethiopia, for, I think of the motherland*
*I think of the originators, my ancestors, and their demise*
*Due to others with recessive genes, and also recessive eyes*
*I think of how people make-believe every other color is worth more*
*BROWN EYES symbolize the beginning, the genesis, the core*

*As I look into all these eyes, one thing I truly see*
*Is how America has programmed most eyes to be as blind as can be*
*I see the future and what could be, If the consciousness would rise*
*If someone like me could give people vision*
*And they could see like I see through these eyes...*

DIARY OF A BLACK MAN....

# HOW BLAK?

BLAK.... How BLAK is really BLAK ?
And who has the right to really attack ?
Only those who truly know for a fact
They are the personification of... BLAK

Our ancestors died, never thinking of BLAK as pride
But a nasty thing to be hated, meaning dead or burnt inside
AFRICAN, AFRO-AMERICAN and NEGRO all apply
Yet so many brothas and sistahs don't see eye to eye

Is BLAK the calling you feel from the people of long ago ?
The responsibility ? the debt ? YES , I believe so
If you are not willing to struggle, give your life or hack
Hack the pain for true freedom, then YOU AIN'T BLAK !

If our ancestors were alive,
they would tell you themselves
Judging by actions, these BLAKS today
wish they were something else
They justify their self-hatred, but can't hide the fact
If you're not part of the struggle and solution
Then, YOU'RE NOT BLAK !!!

"Integration, man" ,"Love thy enemy" and "peace"
Is the way some will tell you all this hatred will cease
Everybody wants freedom and equality
But don't nobody really care
Just like everybody wants to get to heaven
But don't nobody want to DIE to get there
These BLAKS of today wouldn't even be alive
Had our ancestors NOT stuck together to survive
But nowadays when it's convenient
Brothas and sistahs will come around
As if it's a chore, with a sigh
they say "I'm down"
Not understanding at any time
what they TRULY lack
The proper knowledge of self
Which in turn, makes you BLAK

A NIGGER, ILL-BRED, ASS-KISSING, COLORED, FOOL

DIARY OF A BLACK MAN....

Who has the white man's education
Through graduating from his schools
Are ALL that seem to be in these United States
Filled with disgust, disloyalty and self-hate
"What have you been smokin'?"
Oh, I see the situation
White philosophies, ideologies
History and integration
I guess we're all hitting the pipe
Smoking our own form of this "American" crack
So, look in the mirror and ask yourself:

# HOW BLAK?

DIARY OF A BLACK MAN....

Like a flower, one comes
Destined to expand
Developing gradually, inch by inch
Rising above the land
Sprout one does, slowly but surely
Once beyond the dirt
Preparing to flourish amongst the exquisite
In the garden of Mother Earth

Amazingly radiant, one exhibits
Novel assortments of color
Captivatingly in tune with one's surroundings
And expressive unlike any other
One buds then blooms, reaching maximum growth
In spring, summer and fall
Until winter creeps in slowly and smoothly
Bringing a halt to it all...

Watch as one's stem and structure softens
Steadily with each passing day
The petals thin out and the luster diminishes
Until its beauty has gone away
Declining, descending, slumping and drooping
Until the eventual drop
When calm and peaceful, tranquil and still
The surface one lays atop

Returning, melting, into the soil
One placidly goes
Until vanished is all remnants of life
Visible not long ago
Then miraculously peeping through the ground
Appears an itty, bitty stem
And as the sun rises and seasons change

DIARY OF A BLACK MAN....

Mother Nature starts the whole process again...

# THIS STRANGE LAND

Wandering, drifting, my minds often goes
Through big, plentiful forests and golden meadows
On high mountain tops and clear blue streams
To distant beaches, my mind often dreams
I see creatures such as the humming bird
And at night, large owls and crickets are heard
Creating scenarios unreal and unplanned
Due to my placement in this strange land

I walk down the streets in lively downtown
As I stroll aimlessly, I'm consumed with sounds
A couple kissing gently, with arms swinging back and forth
A storekeeper washing windows and sweeping his porch
A transient pleading for some loose coins
Buses and cars, engines and horns
High heels and platforms, feet kicking tin cans
All hurriedly stomping throughout this strange land

I think of my ancestors who never conceived
The thought of brown and yellow maple leaves

*As they lived in a beautiful paradise of their own*
*With sights and sounds, to me, unknown*
*While lions elephants and beautiful butterflies*
*Filled their terrain and flawless skies*
*Until abducted with chains bound to their hands*
*To create what I know as THIS STRANGE LAND*

DIARY OF A BLACK MAN....

# IF I must DIE

Now I awake from a deep sleep
And I pray to God my soul he keeps
If I should die before my people awake
I pray another man like myself he makes...

If I should die, say, tomorrow morn
I pray that day another soldier is born
One who will B-conscious and willing to die
Die for the struggle and the people, just as I...

If I must die for one reason or another
Before my time, may it be for one of my brothers
Not because of gang violence nor any other color
Than BLAK and the land we know as the mother

If I die, I know God has planned it
Knowing I've done all I could do on this planet
Ancestors before me, in a similar fashion
Were taken away, without GOD even askin'

So if I have to go, if it's a must
If ashes must return to ashes, and dust to dust
Then PLEASE, PLEASE, PLEASE, Don't let me die in vain
Though some brothas and sistahs will call me insane
And others will say, I shouldn't have done what I did
Not understanding what it's like, to fully give
I pray to God, someday, awake and eye to eye
My people will finally stand, even if I must die....

Leader after leader has been attacked and executed

DIARY OF A BLACK MAN....

In the media and by the government, until either dead or diluted
While most of my people just went on with their lives
Not thinking about the children, or the leaders' wives'
Not even thinkin' about the fact that every leader represents
The whole, the body, the multitude, to the establishment
So PLEASE God, if only one wish you EVER grant I
PLEASE WAKE MY PEOPLE UP.... Even if I MUST DIE !!!

DIARY OF A BLACK MAN....

# SISTAH, SISTAH

Sistah, my sistah, what's up with you ?
The CREATOR knows you've got to be strong, with all that you've been through
This world owes you alot, giving birth to the hue-man race
Though some of your children oftentimes spit in your face
And some of your children, even wish you were erased
For, obviously they despise you and have forgotten their place

It was you, the first motha, who gave birth to all the leaders
The fighters, the bleeders, the liars and the cheaters
The ones who wish to disgrace you and even exploit you
The ones jealous of your power, who wish to destroy you
Just like your sistah "Nature", Damn, she's been a good mother !
And the kings of Ethiopia and Egypt, the original man, your brotha
See how they try to divide you, get inside you ?
Confuse the whole world, enslave you and hide you ?
They place your brothas in the jails and in the slums
Plus make into a wasteland the sacred place you came from

Sistah, my sistah, I feel what you feel
Watching your brothas, your motha and your fatha killed
Watching rape and miscegenation
Change the faces of our nation
Change the ideologies, create a bunch of fools
Deceived, dishonored, disgusted and taught to disrespect you

I know livin' is hard, doin it on your own
Raisin' the nation's strong and proud, with no fatha in the home
But don't turn on your brotha now
For freedom or death is his vow
And the world has a different plan
A different agenda, when it comes to your man

I know with alot of brothas, you can't communicate
But don't give into you enemy, show love not self-hate
Be that queen you've always been, be that motha of the universe

Be that strong sistah, that lady of GOD
And remember...    you came first !!!

# DAMN!!!

DAMN I say, as I look around
At Blak people acting like a bunch of clowns
Don't they know that it's all a game...
And that they'll still be slaves, even when in fame ?

DAMN I say, to all my brothas
Doggin sistahs and dating others
Don't they know it's a BIG mistake...
Trying to trust a race of female snakes ?
Don't they know, for heaven's sake...
A white-washed, mixed-up baby is all they'll make !

How shall we ever get it together...
If our African children are taught, lighter is better ?
And straighter is prettier, and whiter is brighter...
How will they ever grow to be fighters ?
Yea, they'll fight, maybe even in some wars
But it won't be Africans they'll be fighting for...
They'll fight FOR oppression,
They'll fight AGAINST the slave
Claiming "Massa will be good to ya..."
"If you just behave"

DAMN I say, DAMN, DAMN, DAMN, DAMN !!!
Since when was it better for sistahs
To be with a WHITE man ?

DIARY OF A BLACK MAN....

He'll never love her correctly,
He'll never understand...
He only wants to possess her and undress her
Because she's African....

DAMN Blak people, why won't you see ?
Never, ever will they dare to let us go free
Never, ever will they dare
To admit what they've done...
Never, ever will they tell their plans
And true feelings...     from day one

Envy, oh envy the mighty race
Wish, oh wish they could take our place
Mathematics, architecture
And ALL the sciences across the board...
Came from a place and a people
Now being ignored...

DAMN I say about these fools
Being exploited in sports
Making millions on tracks and fields
Indoor and outdoor courts

Don't they know they need a back-up plan ?
Don't they know that the time is at hand ?
Don't they know they'd better invest ?
Invest in the future of the race
From which they were blessed...

Instead these "NEGROES" want to integrate

DIARY OF A BLACK MAN....

Put sushi, steak and shrimp upon their plates
When we ALL came from the same Motherland
And...
Until we are   ALL free, Until we can ALL eat
Until we can ALL see
Until we control our own destiny
Until none of us are in poverty
Until we all have college degrees
Until Africa has the new technology   AND;
Until the tell our TRUE history
The only reply you'll ever hear from me
Is:            DAMN !!!
What is up with this AMERICAN-African ?

DIARY OF A BLACK MAN....

# L.A.

Genocidal tendencies are what most
Upon this coast, tend to practice
Yet the masses of the population know not why
Or fail to recognize
The true root of the problem at hand
But me ? I understand...

Beautiful be the sun,
In this forever hot and bothered
City, whose founding fathers
Weren't the first to discover
A place already inhabited by others
That they did not see as their brothers

Kill or be killed was the name
Of this colonial, fight for power, materialistic game
While so many indigenous asked
Why these settlers REALLY came...

Pre-L.A. "ghetto gang-bangers"
One might suggest or state
And their mental state
Had already concealed children to comes' fates
Establishing this region, on the premise of hate...

Now graffiti smothered walls
Painted with hieroglyphics of death
Are like the icing upon a cake of old attitudes
About survival of the most determined, destructive group
Known as a gang...
But where did they REALLY learn how to bang ?
When it sure wasn't a Latino or Blak thang...

As people of color scramble in this "city of dreams"
Damn it seems, like something or someone just ain't right
As so many spectate BLAK on BLAK, Brown on Brown
And BLAK on Brown fights...
When those involved need to unite...AGAINST THE WHITES
!!!

As the thought of Beverly Hills
Sends chills, up the spines
Of those left behind, in this rate race
A minute group of tokens secure themselves a place
As the rest of their communities look at them with disgrace
As if to say "How dare you spit in our face !!!"

But everybody knows, the media controls
Everything you hear and see, so don't rely on T.V.
To solve the problems that exist in the hood
For, right around the corner
They're planning your mental and physical destruction
In HOLLYWOOD...

However, nobody REALLY cares, and I swear
If it wasn't for the beaches
Even though the water is polluted
And the forever shining sun
That puts its rays on everyone
I TRULY believe everybody and their mother would have a gun...

But then again, entertainment and sports
Where exploited are people of all sorts
Has a big affect on one's thoughts
About what's hot and what's not
Who's trashy, who's flashy and who's rich
Plus who's considered the Hip-Hop buzzword:

DIARY OF A BLACK MAN....

A " BITCH"
Plus too many other things to list
That keep people of color materialistic
And too obsessed with wealth to raise their fists
And RESIST !!!

This problem will never, ever
By itself go away
And future generations will be forced to pay
All because so many slept, wept,
But still kept
Being unconscious of their plight
On the west coast
Especially in the County of...
And the City of...      L.A.
WHERE GENOCIDAL TENDENCIES ARE THE NORM....IN THEIR PUREST FORM.

DIARY OF A BLACK MAN....

# SMOKED

I turned on the T.V. the other day and saw an ANTI-smoking ad
One aimed at African-Americans, saying our people had it bad
Then I thought about it, and realized...Damn, you know it's a fact
It's really hard in America, when you're poor and BLAK

THEY'VE GOT A CONSPIRACY, A CAMPAIGN, A WAR GOING ON...
A PREMEDITATED PLOT TO DESTROY YOU, OR AT LEAST MAKE SURE YOU'RE GONE...

So naturally, I wanted to see some proof
So, I went and bought some magazines
I looked in Ebony, Jet and Essence thinking, "I see what they mean"
I looked in Cosmopolitan, Vogue and others
Other white magazines and knew
If you're BLAK, you'll see THREE TIMES as many ads
Meaning the companies are targeting you...
Meaning the genocidal tendencies we ALL seem to acquire
Come from SUBLIMINAL MESSAGES
From the government and those up higher...

When I'm traveling in suburbia
I see libraries and health-food stores
Yet, in ethnic parts of towns
It's tobacco and alcohol billboards
Which tells me deep down in my heart
If you're BLAK, life is a joke
You're subjected to all kinds of negative images
And taught to drink and smoke

Billions of dollars are spent on ads
While the cigarette companies

DIARY OF A BLACK MAN....

Deny their affects on your health
Like Cancer and Lung Disease
It's scary to think of what happens
When you offer someone a couple of "mill"
Like BLAK owners of BLAK magazines and businesses
Who sell out our futures, while our children foot the bill

When I think of all the companies and agencies
Who try so hard to put my people to rest
I get so stressed out, I say DAMN...
I think I NEED a cigarette !!!

DIARY OF A BLACK MAN....

# GONE WITH THE WIND

Winds of confusion blow around me
As I wonder what my future holds
The weather in my life seldom changes
And the wind stays forever cold

A product of my environment
I'm only as good as that place
Which belongs to me always
No matter the distance and space

Fear of the unknown often traps me
And makes me frequently want to stay
Though deep in my heart, I know I must push
For, upward is the only way

Tears run down my cheeks often
As I think of those who came before
Only to fall short of full flight
And for that reason, like an eagle I soar

Forever circling or so it seems
Gaining momentum, strength and speed
Hoping someday to be remembered
For my dreams, my thoughts and my deeds

I want to leave something behind

***Before it all comes to an end***
***And like ashes to ashes and dust to dust***
***I too am gone with the wind...***

# STRUGGLE

*Struggle... Life is but a mere struggle...*

Strugglin' with that first word "mom " or "dad"
Strugglin' to learn your ABC's
Strugglin' to take that first step
Strugglin' to learn "Thank You" and "Please"

*Life is but a mere struggle...It's true... struggle, struggle, struggle...*

Strugglin' to get straight A's in school
Strugglin' to learn how to ask a girl out
Strugglin' with that first pimple
Strugglin' with that first paper route

*Life is nothing but a struggle...Struggle, struggle, struggle, struggle, struggle...*
*Man, I'm so sick of strugglin'....*

Strugglin' just to maintain , Go to school and have a girl
Strugglin' not to get caught up in drugs
Strugglin' being BLAK in a WHITE world
Strugglin' to graduate from college
And find out what you'll do with that knowledge
Strugglin' to find a decent job to raise a family on
Strugglin' to fit in and be in the right crowd
Strugglin' to get those proper promotions
Strugglin' with being denied
Strugglin' to STILL stand BLAK and proud

*Struggle DAMN    IT, Struggle !!!    Life is but a mere struggle...*

Strugglin' to understand why BLAKS don't stick together
Strugglin' to understand the government of the United States
Strugglin' to understand the differences between prejudice and racism
Strugglin' to deal with self-hate
Strugglin' to understand why the average WHITE family makes more than you do
Even with your college degree
Strugglin' to understand why you can NEVER retire

DIARY OF A BLACK MAN....

*Strugglin' to understand this society*

*Strugglin' to put money away for your kids*
*So they don't have to struggle as you did*
*Strugglin' to teach them before you die*
*That strugglin' is a necessary part of life*

*Struggle, struggle, struggle, struggle, struggle, struggle, STRUGGLE !!!*
*Life is but a mere struggle...*

*Struggle's bred, it's inherent*
*It's coded in the cells deep within you*
*And as long as life is a struggle for BLAK America........THE STRUGGLE MUST CONTINUE !!!*

DIARY OF A BLACK MAN....

# THE DREAM

I have a dream that one day an African baby will be born
And not looked upon by the world with scorn
That one day in school every boy and girl
Will learn the truth about Africa, and its contributions to the world
I HAVE A DREAM...

I have a dream that someday God will control every nation
And BLAKS will receive apologies and reparations
That WHITES will finally let Africa be restored
By vacating it and ceasing to pimp it like a whore
I HAVE A DREAM...

I have a dream that BLAKS and WHITES will finally find out
What Martin Luther's dream was REALLY about
I HAVE SEEN HIS DREAM...

As in the United States and the rest of the globe
European domination continues to control
But BLAKS still dream... Africans still dream...

Africans dream to finally control their country
And not be subjected to poverty.... That's their dream
They dream they will able to live, think and dress
To worship and exist as they did before Europe's conquest
They have this dream...

This unbelievably, is the BIG dream also
Of African people's everywhere, even the so-called "Negro"
In America, his immediate dreams are much more complicated
Due to the fact he's been a 400 year native
But he still has a dream...

He has a dream that he will someday get recognition
For his laborious tasks, loyalty and inventions...
That he will be able to finally control his community
And not be called a racist for promoting BLAK unity
THIS IS HIS DREAM...

He has a dream that his children will control their destinies
Without fear of government harassment and police brutality

DIARY OF A BLACK MAN....

That inter-racial relationships and full-scale integration
Will be an afterthought, following first, a strong BLAK nation
That Martin and Malcolm's dreams and views
Will not be used to deceive, watered down or misconstrued
The American-African isn't as naive as he seems
For he also knows the struggle, pain, blood and sweat
It takes to obtain this dream…

He has a dream, we have dreams and THIS IS THE DREAM…
SO…DREAM ON..

# WHERE IS MY QUEEN ?

*Let me as you something... WHERE IS MY QUEEN ?*
*Where is my "Eve" for whom I can be "Adam" ?*
*My "Mary" for whom I can be both "Joseph" and "Jesus" ?*
*WHERE IS MY QUEEN ?*

*Where is my strong, proud, fighter through ANYTHING ?*
*Friend and mother of nature and the animals ?*
*My "Bambi"?*
*WHERE IS MY QUEEN ?*

*Where is my fiery-eye, ice cold, solid as a rack*
*Warm hearted, sweet, nurturing, passionate, friendly confidant ?*
*WHERE IS MY QUEEN ?*

*Where is that unmoving, unshakable, universal*
*Hair not straight, but perfectly curled*
*Sometimes unmanageable, coarse ,tangled and even nappy*
*But all the time, NATURAL...*

*Skin; bronze, brown , caramel, brown sugar, dark chocolate*
*Smooth as if to be leather, wonderful, moist even without lotion*
*Warrior if need be, but POWERFUL always*
*Amazon, with whom all other women compare themselves...*
*WHERE IS MY QUEEN ?*

*Where is my Nefertiti*
*Controlling whole lands far and near with one finger*
*Voice of pure melody, making birds sing with every syllable*
*Seasons change with every sentence*
*And winds blow with every breath*
*Outlasting any other ever heard of...*
*WHERE IS MY QUEEN ?*

*Where is my Cleopatra*
*My queen of all queens, only second to God*
*Sitting right next to the father in spirituality*

DIARY OF A BLACK MAN....

*Giving unto herself, while never forgetting*
*Who she is, what she is and why she is*
*The strong raiser of the children and teacher of all...*
*WHERE IS MY QUEEN ?*


*I have not seen her yet...*
*Has she fell from her throne ?*
*Has she suddenly got amnesia ?*
*Has something or some one tainted her ?*
*WHERE IS MY QUEEN ?*

*Oh, how I wait for the day I can find her*
*Hold her and caress her...*
*WHERE IS MY QUEEN ?*

*Where is she now that we've arrived in America ?*
*Has someone took her ?    Raped her ?   Reshaped her ?*
*Made her not love me as much ?*
*Has she lost all of the pride I used to love so well ?*
*WHAT HAS HAPPENED TO MY QUEEN ?*

*Where is my resilient, sagacious, marvelous,*
*Magnificent, treacherous yet still sensitive,*
*One in a trillion, sistah to justice, equality and fairness*
*Enemy to evil unrighteousness and dishonesty*
*Motivated by love to conquer all sinister plots and people*
*WHERE IS MY QUEEN ?*

*Well, in America or wherever she may be*
*I shall find her if I must search forever*
*I shall find my Harriet Tubman, my Rosa Parks*
*My Betty Shabazz, my Sistah Soljah*
*My Sojourner Truth, my Assata Shakur*
*My mother of civilization, still and always*
*My queen of the universe, holder of all truths*
*First nurse, kind but sturdy, uncompromising*
*Woman of the world, in the world and on top of the world*
*My Asiatic, every corner of the world*
*POPULATING THE EARTH BY HERSELF*
*African, original queen...*


**DIARY OF A BLACK MAN....**

*Please stand up, wherever you are...*
*For, your king has returned !!!*

DIARY OF A BLACK MAN....

# RAIN

*As God cleans the earth,*
*With his heavenly showers*
*A many feel his nurturing,*
*As they bathe within his power*
*Washed from sight are the disposals*
*And wastes of yesterday*
*As the refreshing smell of purity,*
*Takes all others away*

*Revitalized and replenished,*
*Appears nature for a day or so*
*As down the gutter, into the drain,*
*All wickedness flows*
*Many find awesomeness*
*And mystic within the rain*
*While others find shelter and a guise*
*To hide their inner pain...*

*Between the raindrops, you will find,*
*Lies one's inner-fears*
*Frustrations, anguish, misery and heartache*
*Expressed in the form of tears...*
*When it rains, so many stroll,*
*Releasing their silent sobs*
*Soaked faces result not from the weather*
*As much as menial jobs..*

*Being kept down, deprived and dehumanized*
*Makes one often feel*
*Emotions and thoughts, for survival*
*Must be all concealed*
*And its for this reason, a many souls*

**With burdens upon their brains
Wait patiently to release all the pain
While walking in the rain....**

DIARY OF A BLACK MAN....

# "FUCKED"

You know, BLAK people love fuckin'
Have you ever noticed how much we love to fuck ?

We fucked our own when the WHITE man came to Africa
And sold them for a little bit of gold
We fucked over the slaves in the field trying to free us
How ? We fuckin' told

Buffalo soldiers fucked up the "Indians"
Who used to be our friends
And we've fucked up every movement
Almost as soon as it began

Now we fuck off jobs and fuck off money
Even more than we make
Plus we fuck somebody every chance we get
Not to mention how we're so fuckin' fake

In a fuckly fashion, it's our own fuckin' people
We fuck over the most
Fuckin' up shit like some bad motherfuckers
On each and every coast

Man, we're so fuckin' fucked up
We can't even see straight
Most of us would fuck over God for a dollar
And fuck up our fuckin' fates
                    BUT WAIT....

If we could change the "F" to "S"
And instead of FUCK... SUCK
Just imagine what that would do for our people
 And how that would change our luck ...

DIARY OF A BLACK MAN....

We'd be able to suck up all the knowledge
That we get in school
Instead of fuckin' off our lives
By getting fucked up to be cool

We'd suck up the billions our people make
Instead of always spending
And we'd think as one and suck others in
Like Africa did in the beginning

Just imagine what it would be like
To intake or to consume
To always be the most educated
And richest in every room

As it stands right now, BLAKS are at the bottom
Of every single pile
Cause' others have sucked up all of our culture
Talents and our style

BLAKS NEED TO WAKE THE FUCK UP
And quit fuckin' around
Quit suckin' the WHITE man's dick
And suck in the sights and sounds

Suck in air, suck in actions
And words of the past
Suck in spirituality, suck in God
And suck it in hard and fast

For, if we don't, then our people
Will always and forever be stuck
In a fucked situation
And in a world that really, truly sucks...

## NOW THAT'S FUCKED !!!

**DIARY OF A BLACK MAN....**

# CAN WE LOVE?

Can we talk ? Can we as one communicate?
Without raising our voices or showing inner-self hate ?

Can we make decisions ? Make future goals to reach ?
And stay focused, while each other, we take the time to teach ?

Can we listen to each others needs ? Can we lend an ear ?
To concerns, fears and frustrations, that someone needs to hear ?

CAN WE LOVE each other, the way we need to ?
And realize with love comes strength, and with that we'll make it through

Can we stop all the negativity, and just take the time to see...
That attacking each other is self-distructive and will bring an end to you and me ?

Can we learn from our past mistakes and make a vow...
To stand by each other 'til the end, no matter when, where or how ?

Can we trust in each other, and give ourselves a chance ?
Not assuming the worst, or having preconceptions about one another in advance ?

Can we smile ? Think positively, laugh and even cry ?
Give all that our minds and hearts can give , until the day we die ?

Tell me.... # CAN WE LOVE ?

# BITCH

*You know so many brothas, call our sistahs "hoes"*
*And claim they're all BITCHES who wear too tight clothes*

*So I say, "Hey Brothas, be conscious of what you say"*
*"Who was it not long ago, who told them to dress that way?"*

*"I remember when sistahs wouldn't show, what now you see"*
*"And was it not the brothas, who showed them and told them what was sexy?"*

*" But now want them to change, you exclaim, and do it over night!!!"*
*However, would you comply?   Changing in you what isn't right?"*

*"My sistahs say; lazy and selfish...Thinking he's God's gift to the world"*
*"The black man is, and due to weakness, he prefers a dumb WHITE girl..."*

*"Is this true? Or lie they do ? Tell me is there validity?"*
*"To the statements made by sistahs, claiming what they perceive"*

*"Well, I can honestly step outside, look in, and attest to the fact..."*
*"Brothas and sistahs BOTH got problems and are BOTH pots calling the kettles BLACK"*

*Neither side is better and neither side is worse"*
*"And neither side can solve the problem, Until both Simultaneously reverse..."*
*"So brothas, when you speak on your sistahs ...What you REALLY do.."*
*"Is speak on your mother and yourselves, for, your sistah is part of you..."*

*"What you can do, is knowledge your sistahs, for, some of them haven't a clue..."*
*"For, you can never know your full potential, until you understand what you've been reduced to"*

*"Besides, there's a mate for everybody, regardless of ones taste..."*
*"It's all a simple matter of just looking in the right place"*

*"For, there's plenty of brothas and sistahs out there"*

DIARY OF A BLACK MAN....

*"Who share your points of view"*

*"But there's also plenty of brothas and sistahs who feel
The REAL BITCH is a brotha like you"*

# FREE

As I look outside my window
At birds flying by
I wonder what they were
In their past lives

They had to be something distraught
Distressed and unhappy
To come back in this life
As something so free

A nest up in the sky is their home
On the branch of a tree
In Mother Nature's arms
Amongst the clouds, they love to be

MY hypothesis is that
They were BLAK long ago
And in justice, when they died
God made them free as the winds that blow

Maybe they were slaves
Or in the Civil War
They could've been around during reconstruction
Or freedom riders before

I don't know, but my hypothesis
In my mind is without doubt
Wouldn't only an ex-slave for the winter
Want to fly south ?

What better way to live your life

DIARY OF A BLACK MAN....

*Than to have wings*
*Flying all over the world*
*Seeing millions of people and things*

*If and when I die*
*I hope God makes me*
*Like those who now soar the earth*
*Relaxed and finally free*

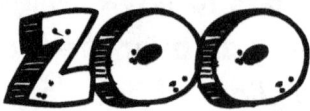

Have you ever been to the zoo
And thought about the politics ?
Man, I see all those animals caged
And in my heart know it's sick...

How can someone come to this land
And chase and kill all the animals off...
Rob, steal and rape it for its resources
Yet claim to have a heart that's soft

How do you justify the killing of things
Plus the control and capture of all the rest
By those claiming to be a people of God
In submission to him and blessed...

I see animals in zoos that should be made free
So the earth they can freely roam
In their natural habitat, Living off the land
Not in cages, but their original homes...

Look at the indigenous in this country,
They were killed or put on reservations
As for the African, it was the same scenario
Except for us, it was the plantation...

Now it's the ghetto or prison
Either one is about the same
Proving that every type of original
Has been placed in a zoo of some name

For observation and entertainment
Or they have been hunted and killed for sport
By a fascist, a maniac, a madman
A DEVIL who shall be tried in God's court...

DIARY OF A BLACK MAN....

He knows what he's doing, he sits back and plots
He smiles and laughs, you should see him
While he even puts people's cultures in zoos
Known to most as museums...

So fight if you can, to stop this man
Boycott museums and zoos
For, if you don't, before you know it
The next exhibit on display will be you...

DIARY OF A BLACK MAN....

# Slave Song

From the days you brought me on ships
To the days you beat me with whips
When in the fields I worked all day long
I sang and sang my slave songs

From the time you finally let me free
To the days I fought for this country
Overseas in Germany and Vietnam
I sang and sang my slave songs

From the church pews both day and night
To the marches and protests for Civil Rights
I declared I 'd keep movin' on
And I kept on singing my slave songs

DIARY OF A BLACK MAN....

Though they've changed throughout the years
As jazz, blues and gospel once told my fears
But now it's R&B and Rap 'til the break o'dawn
I continue to sing my slave songs

# NFL

*I used to love football*
*I used to like the N.F.L*
*That is, until I became conscious*
*After that, it became a living hell...*

*RUN, NIGGAH, RUN...*
*Sell your inner soul*
*Make a couple million*
*While the WHITE man keeps control*
*Kind of like a SLAVE*
*Preconditioned to react*
*You can play for somebody else's team*
*But can't own one, if you're BLAK*

*The N.F.L. makes so much money, it's a damn shame*
*How BLAK people run up and down the field, for mere penny change*

*We buy the most N.F.L. products*
*But where does the money go ?*
*To the owners who invest AGAINST us*
*And keep us in ghettos*
*For, if you think about it , it's perfect*
*See, one of the ONLY ways to get out*
*Is to play football for one of THEIR teams*
*And that's what exploitation is all about*

*The brothas who truly try to help their people*
*Don't stay around to long*
*They get drafted and dogged, until they get the message*
*That what they're doing is wrong*
*As for the rest ...*
*you know the story*
*In the right circles*
*Once they get the glory*
*The fame was already predicted*
*So the WHITE man assumed*
*He'd take care of them in high school and college*
*By sending WHITE girls to their rooms...*

*But if BLAKS just got the knowledge*
 *Instead of playing sports*
*Just for ONE generation...*
*We'd have so much more*

DIARY OF A BLACK MAN....

*If we'd quit spending money on thing we don't need*
*And started making decisions collectively*
*We'd change our plight and love ourselves*
*Plus, we'd own our own N.F.L*

*For, it's US one pays to see*
*Flow up the fields speedily*
*And it's US that makes the teams*
*So much a part of the "American Dream"*
*And it's US who gives a team it's fame*
*Making and Breaking every record in the game*
*So B-Conscious of what you're buying*
*And what they REALLY sell*
*Our independence or servitude ?*
*Within the N.F.L... Negro Football League or New form of Labor ?*
*YOU DECIDE*

DIARY OF A BLACK MAN....

# PART

**Part,** Part , Part, Part, **Everybody is made up of parts...**

PART THIS AND *part that,* Part skinny **and** part FAT
**Everybody is made up of parts...**

**But you know what I have recently found
People play up WHITENESS and put down the** BROWN
**If you call somebody ethnic or** BLAK, **what you instantly get
Is "Well I'm part** GERMAN, EUROPEAN, ITALIAN **OR** IRISH
**As if to say they're better, or they've got a purer heart
Thinking their** ETHNICITY **is only as good, as their** UN-ethnic **part**

**I meet** BLAK **people who say, " Who me ? I'm** mixed"
**As if one's perception instantly changes, and everything is fixed
They act as if by saying these things, they can change the fact
That being** MULATTO **doesn't make you WHITE, sorry... you're still** BLAK **!!!**

**However, to the WHITE races, most people tend to cling
For, when it comes to** inferiority, **in their minds, it's a** BLAK **thing
So they come up with these justifications, thinking that they're smart
Saying "I'm not this nor** that, **I'm just made up of** parts"

**But what few seem to realize, is that being** AFRICAN
**Means you're** ORIGINAL, **for little do they know, we came before the WHITE man**

**And that being part WHITE or being part anything, what that REALLY means
Is that you come from a** weaker **,** **more recessive gene**

**Now why would one stress this point, or brag about this fact ?**

DIARY OF A BLACK MAN....

It's Africa and DARK SKIN that's HEALTHIER, so why not brag about that ?
But the world has been colonized in most ethnic sections
By groups of people who put emphasis on lighter complexions

They claim all the sciences as THEIR creations, Philosophy, Culture and *Art*
And if you're not conscious, then of course, you'll definitely cling to THEIR part

For, rape and brainwashing, have made a many hate themselves
Doing whatever necessary to appear as something else
They have this false belief, that the world will instantly view
Each individual in the way, that individual wants them to

But what REALLY needs to be done, is to attack those who define
What complexion is good or *bad,* when it comes to the color LINE

Then equality will be reality, for those both light and dark
And people could be secure in themselves, not just secure with one *part*...

DIARY OF A BLACK MAN....

Look around at people and things
At the cricket that chirps and the birds that sing
At the grass, oh so green, the trees, oh so tall
Your environment, the weather... look at it all

While you're looking, you'll notice little things that most don't see
Just stop,stare silently and let your mind be free
Once you do, you'll become conscious of surroundings at all times
And when you see these things again, it'll be with your mind...

I used to take my environment for granted
The political and social seeds that were planted
The subliminal messages seen everyday
That causes people to act in certain ways

So many people walk around like they're dead
With mixed up views and lies in their heads
I guess that comes from teachings and reading fiction books
Fear of reality, which makes your mind not truly look...

Television, newspapers and radios
Program people to BELIEVE, but not to truly know
They say whatever they want, just like the government
And all this countries' patriotic, loyal inhabitants

Mental slavery, yes indeed, for all the rest
Who are fooled by a group of DEVILS, in power through conquest
These predecessors of the original rapists, murderers and crooks
Are just the same, ALL OF THEM, take a minute and just look...

Inferior status based on color, culture and dividends
Seems much like what was experienced by the so-called "Indians"

DIARY OF A BLACK MAN....

Conquer, capture and kill anyone who stands in their way
Was the plan of yesterday, still practiced to this day

So much evil done to so many, all throughout history
Yet so many ignore the facts and follow false beliefs
Thinking now It's different, but awake they should be shook
For, to see clearly, you must B-CONSCIOUS.... so open your mind and .....LOOK !!!

# TIES

WE POSSESS THE TIES THAT BIND
TIES THAT MAKE US ONE
THOUGH SEPARATED THROUGH DIFFERENCES
AND FEARS THAT MAKE US RUN

YOU ARE A PART OF ME
AND I AM A PART OF YOU
THOUGH WE BOTH DENY IT
IN OUR HEARTS WE KNOW ITS TRUE

OUR RELATIONSHIP IS COMPLICATED
AND FULL OF NEGATIVITY
HOWEVER, I STILL LEARN FROM YOU
JUST AS YOU DO FROM ME

TO SEPARATE FROM YOU
SEEMS TO BE ALL BUT RIGHT
YET STAYING WITH YOU AS I'VE BEEN
WILL JUST INTENSIFY OUR FIGHTS

NEVER WILL WE ADMIT
OUR VALUE TO EACH OTHER
JUST AS NEVER SHALL YOU ADMIT
BEING ALSO FROM MY MOTHER

THIS IS WHY THESE TIES THAT BIND
WE WISH WE COULD SEVER
FOR, REGARDLESS OF HOW WE TRY
WE'LL NEVER LIVE PEACEFULLY TOGETHER

CONFUSED AND TRAPPED IN QUITE A DILEMMA
SEEMS TO BE OUR FATES
FILLED WITH LOVE FOR OURSELVES

DIARY OF A BLACK MAN....

**WHILE FOR EACH OTHER, FILLED WITH HATE**

**WE KNOW , DESPITE OUR EFFORTS**
**JUST WHAT GOD HAS PLANNED**
**THERE WILL ALWAYS BE TIES BETWEEN US**
**LIKE THE SEA HAS WITH THE SAND**

DIARY OF A BLACK MAN....

# NEW SHOES

I wear my BLAKNESS openly
Like a new pair of shoes
While other people try to hide it like a scar
Or a juvenile tattoo

Me, I openly show the world just what God has made
The beauty, the hue the chromosome,
The melanin, the shade

With my skin comes a culture
So original, so vast
It tells the meaning of all things around me
And links them to the past

Others who wear this badge of humanity
Wish to take it off
Having no idea of what they possess
Nor the value of such a loss

So I must be the parader of BLAKNESS
Walking with pride and joy
I realize only I can bring honor to it
And every BLAK girl and boy

With it, I shall show the world
What it used to mean

DIARY OF A BLACK MAN....

**What it STILL stands for and what it WILL stand for
Each and every time it's seen**

**I exclaim to everyone, everywhere
"Boy have I got news..."
BLAK is beautiful, Blak is original
As I wear it like a new pair of shoes**

DIARY OF A BLACK MAN....

# DARK SHADOWS

Shadowy days and shadowy nights
Stuck in the shadows, that is my plight
Never to escape or even retreat
From the dark shadows that constantly surround me

Life often looks so dark and dim
And is never understood from the outside looking in
But nevertheless, I still go on
Drifting through the dark, never seeing dawn

Nobody knows what it's like in the dark
The mere thought of one's existence
Is no walk through the park
My emotions are painted in blues, BLAKS and greys
With fluorescent undertones, highlighted by a purple haze

Though I walk through this darkness, I still am seen
But only as an animal, who acts cold and mean
For, to the rest of the world, who knows not my plight
Just a creature I am and a shadow in the night...

# MY SOUL

In the depths of hell, my person dwells
But above and beyond , my mind sails
As my flesh is confined to a human hell
My spirituality and knowledge makes my brain swell

Shackle my body, if you must
Defamate my character, look at me with disgust
And even if you do, I still shall grow
For, despite you efforts, the truth I still know

My soul is with God and has always been
From before your chastisements, when my life began
And when It's all over, said and done
My soul shall rise like the morning sun

Your actions shall never affect me so much
That my inner-being shall be negatively touched
I shall always see past your unrighteous ways
For, in the arms of God, I eternally lay

# RELAXED

*You know brothas and sistahs are so relaxed
Many of them have forgotten what it means to be BLAK
I see brothas and sistahs who will disrespect
Everything for which our ancestors broke their necks*

*Materialism and wealth seem to be the main goals
Of these people whose own destiny, they don't control
White-washed brothas and sistahs, today you will find
Will relax their hair, due to relaxed minds*

*These brothas and sistahs ain't even up on the facts
They need to get off their butts, instead of being so relaxed
As they waste their money trying to look good
White people are investing AGAINST the hood*

*While Timberland and Nike make a billion or two*

*BLAKS are struggling and hustling without a clue*
*White liberals have instilled deep down in BLAKS*
*"You're free now, we're all equal, so just relax..."*

*And they fell for it, they fell for the trap*
*No justice, no peace, yet pay the same tax*
*As they wage a war against Civil Rights*
*BLAKS still stand by, instead of stand and fight*

*BLAKS STILL believe things will eventually change*
*While every other ethnic group looks at them strange*
*They'll be caught off guard, when WHITES bring slavery back*
*Why ? because they were unconscious and so damn relaxed...*

# DO OR DIE

GENOCIDE
      *HOMICIDE*
          SUICIDE...
**No blacks side by side**            Getting sprayed with human pesticides
    NO BLACK PRIDE

    NO TOUR GUIDE
**THROUGH THIS** HELL **WHERE** devils **RESIDE**...
   ANCESTORS CRIED
**THE WHITE MAN LIED**
*Brothas have died*
   And mothers STILL cry...
    **As, in a** slave ship, **on a high tide**...
*Africans came to labor in the hot sun and fry*
          Making cotton KING,
with a   *blue sky*
   Putting the WHITE man on high...

DIARY OF A BLACK MAN....

But now blaks wonder why **THEY CAN'T SURVIVE**
*And the WHITE man replies:*     **"Don't blame it on I"**
But everybody knows BLAKS aren't satisfied
**As the ghetto, most of us occupy**
*Where all tragedies are magnified*
**By a media, that doesn't identify**
*With a people for whom* REVOLUTION
*Is simply a case of...*
**DO** OR *DIE !!!*

# PROGRESS

As I walk down the streets
Or hang with my buddies on the block
I observe people doing what they do
And I realize:     WE MAKE NO PROGRESS...

As I turn on the television
And receive images in my home
I notice, African-Americans are on t.v. more
But still I say:     WE MAKE NO PROGRESS...

As I go to the movies or the mall
And watch my brothas and sistahs' spending habits
I ask myself:     WHEN WILL WE MAKE PROGRESS ?

As I listen to politicians
Who represent the BLAK community
Yet experience in the hood
A lack of unity
I think to myself: DAMN! NO PROGRESS...

Everything Africans have in America
Is a small proportion to that of whites
And, as we have gained and earned more...
So have they...     But
Still we sit at the same proportional level

**Meaning:** **NO PROGRESS !!!**

**QUIT DANCING, COMEDY CLUBBIN', RESTAURANT GRUBBIN',
BUYIN', CHEATIN', LYIN', DYIN'.....
And let's
MANUFACTURE, DISTRIBUTE, EDUCATE, STIMULATE, UNIFY
And..         PROGRESS....    LET'S PROGRESS !!!**

DIARY OF A BLACK MAN....

# WORDS

Words are nothing but mere symbols
Put together to form statements
Words are powerful when combined right
And can leave others staring in amazement

Words are one of the chief devices
Used in expression and communication
Spirituality, art, and even music
But most of all in education

Words can bring forth visions from the mind
Giving one deep insight
Control they can and even condemn
Or be weapons with which one fights

All in all, words are basically tools
That everyone should possess
Use and abuse, if one must
All in the name of progress

Manipulated and maneuvered correctly
Words can set one free
Or they can tie one down, leave one gagged and bound
When one hasn't the ability to read

Words, words, I love words
And you should love them too
Utilize them and monopolize them, you should
Or do with them what I do...

I use words to bring to life
Thoughts and images of long ago
Ancestors I conjure and revive
I bring back to life, old revolutionary souls

Ones that never got to see justice

DIARY OF A BLACK MAN....

Freedom nor equality
Ones that roam, linger and dangle
Never, ever truly free

With my words, I tell the world
What the CREATOR really wanted
And how the earth right now, by evil demons
Is truly and thoroughly haunted


What we've been, where we've been
And all the things that we went through
Plus, how we as a people, today
Can start our lives anew

Words I take and I transform
Into steaks and stab devils through the heart
I create, I use eloquence, diction and diversity
To show the whole world that I'm smart

I bring the world my experiences
My dreams and of course my plight
My fears, nightmares and my journeys
My soul, my spirit and my life

With my words, Hell, I start a REVOLUTION
Motivating one to stand sturdy and strong
Telling the oppressor and his children
"We've been taking this shit far too long"

With my words, I express my passion
My desire, love and devotion
Filled are my words with enormous flavor
Plus various raw emotions

I laugh, I cry, I pain and I anger
And it shows through my use of the pen
For when the world passes me, forgets me and I'm alone
Ink, paper and words are my best friends


DIARY OF A BLACK MAN....

Together we give to the rich, to the poor
The defenseless and to the confined
From the gutters of the ghetto to the belly of the beast
And even the White House gets a piece of my mind

Though if you were to put your ear to the ground
Or in the wind, I shall not be heard
My voice shall carry on, even when I'm gone
How ? Through my arrangement of words...

DIARY OF A BLACK MAN....

# O.J.

You know, despite what most people say
I Don't really fancy or even like O.J.
I don't believe O.J. is actually good for you
I'm more into something like prune or grape juice
I'm not one for coffee, even with a little cream
It's got to be BLAK, you know what I mean?

I don't even drink milk, but if I did drink some
It would have to be chocolate, get where I'm coming from ?
NO O.J. but maybe apple juice, cider or root beer
No fruit punch, no 7-up and no sprite
It's too light and too clear

You know I don't even like WHITE bread
I've gots to have wheat or rye instead
That's right, no WHITE, always make it wheat
Even if I ate chicken, It would only be DARK meat
For me bronze, brown, BLAK and even tan is O.K.

DIARY OF A BLACK MAN....

**But never ever will you catch me with anything even close
To that of...O.J. !!!**

# SOURCE

Return to your source...
Which is Africa, of course

Must all of these Americanized, Londonized, Europeanized
British, Cuban, Spainish, Brazilianized Africans
Be taken back to Africa, put in chains and branded
For them to understand...
They are nothing more, nothing less, nothing else
But African ?

Must they, too
Be confined to the corn and cotton fields?
Must they be killed...
Before they feel the African inside is real?

What does it take to make them see?
Africa is them, it's you, it's me !!!
Call yourselves what you may
But Africa is not free !!!

What will it take?
The whip burning their backs?
cutting through their skin
Whether dark or light BLAK?

Must they cut their first teeth on pork fat
Tied around their necks ?
Before they learn some kind of respect?

Need they be bought and sold
In the blistering hot and death of cold?
Before they remember not to believe
What, by the WHITE man, they have been told?

What must be done to make ALL men
Women and children of color
Realize we are ALL sisters and brothers
From the same Mother ?

Must the White man again, fully do

DIARY OF A BLACK MAN....

What in the past he's done?
Not only with religion
But most of all, with his guns?

I am African
You are African
They are African
We are...

What will it take to make
The Red-Man
The Yellow-Man,
The Brown-Man
And the BLAK-Man especially...

WHAT IN THE WORLD WILL MAKE THOSE UNFREE FINALLY SEE ?

Africa and ONLY Africa is the key
And what and where we should ALL be...

I am African
You are African
They are African
We are...

# *AFRICA*

# WHATDOUWANTWITHMYSISTAH?

America, America, the land of the free
The multi-cultural melting pot, or so it appears to be
Home of integration, miscegenation and letting the love flow
But before you do all that, there's just one thing I need to know...

WHATDOUWANTWITHMYSISTAH ?
What with her do you intend to do ?
European mongrel, American WHITE man and Neanderthal
Yes...I mean you !!!

What do you want my sistah for ?
What exactly is your plan ?
Control, coercion, deception, and annihilation
Of all that's African ?

Just what do you intend to do with her?
Water her down, Eurocentrisize
And Americanize her mind ?
For, you haven't any REAL culture
You've been stealing ours the whole time...

What can you TRULY give her?
Except maybe an inferiority complex
As you make her more confused about our situation and plight
Through with her, having sex

WHATDOUWANTWITHMYSISTAH ?
You can't make her stronger, just submit
As you try to fill her head with all of that
"Don't hate WHITE people, we can't help our better position in society...
HELL NO, WE'RE NOT GIVING YOU REPARATIONS, There's no racism anymore...
Just erase the color lines..." BULL SHIT !!!

What is it that you want from my sistah ?
Maybe you just want to impregnate her with a bunch of mulatto children
In hopes you can fade us all to white
And deteriorate our thoughts of REVOLUTION and repatriation
As you try to destroy our nation...

DIARY OF A BLACK MAN....

What knowledge of self are you givin' her?
Are you into Afrocentricity and diggin' her?
Or are you just having inferiority flashes
Knowing you came from me?
Knowing you came from she?
Knowing you came from we?
Is it the challenge that makes you be
So attracted to my sistah?
JUST LEAVE HER ALONE !!!
You can do nothing constructive with her
All you want is her for your own...

You're still trying to imitate, fraudulate
Psuedo-create and intimidate
Which all leads up to self-hate
But hold up, WAIT !!!

Recessive genes
Recess, you know what I mean?
We're trying to progress
And fade back to BLAK
So...STEP BACK !!!

As you emasculate the BLAK man
In hopes you can, then be
All that's left for my sistah...

WHATDOUWANTWITHMYSISTAH?
To fill her head with contempt?
You want her as a trophy piece, an acknowledgement
Of your accomplishments...

You can give her NOTHING
For she is all you can NEVER be
God made her "Mother of Civilization"
And put her here to FIGHT White supremacy

Not to cooperate with your plan
To degenerate her King or her Pharaoh
Is your mind really that narrow?
Her spirituality is higher than the clouds
And she flies above you like a sparrow

As you still try to figure us out

DIARY OF A BLACK MAN....

And what our spirituality is REALLY about
And we keep creating, relating and deviating...

WHATDOUWANTWITHMYSISTAH ?
I ask brothas the same thing also, you see
For if a brotha is not mentally and spiritually sound
Then alone, he too should be

As for you, we know your motives and plots
Every since the slave days
For my sistah, you've had the hots

Is it the strength deep within her
That all others lack
Maybe that's why the nannies
Who raised your children were BLAK

I could go on and on but what's the use ?
We both know of your past and present cultural abuse
And now you expect me, expect us
To just let you have our sistah ?
We ain't in chains no more
And we see how in the past you dissed her

So now what you planning to do ?
Some freaky-deeky, modern-day
Turn her out and make her gay
Type stuff ?
Cause we've had enough...

On the real, you know the deal
Just as I know the deal
And I know YOU know the deal
And YOU know I know that YOU know the deal
So my question is still...

# WHATDOUWANTWITHMYSISTAH?
NOTHING... Right, mister ?

DIARY OF A BLACK MAN....

# *GUN CONTROL...*

CAPOW !!! BANG, BANG !!!
SHOOT 'EM UP, RAT-A-TAT-TAT,
KAK-KAK-KAK-KAK-KAK !!!

Everybody's talkin' about gun control
So let's talk about gun control, shall we ?
Everybody wants more gun control
Thinking this will save lives and save souls
GOVERNMENT GUN CONTROL ? Please....come on !!!
There can be no gun control until WE control the guns

Remember with HIS guns, he came and killed the "Indians"
Remember the French-Indian War, need I say more ?

CAPOW !!! BANG, BANG !!!
SHOOT 'EM UP, RAT-A-TAT-TAT,
KAK-KAK-KAK-KAK-KAK !!!

The Apaches, Siouxs, Sitting Bull, Geronimo
Yea, I heard somebody say THEY wanted gun control
The gun has been used in every place on the globe
To capture, convince, contain and control
Gun control? When all is said and done
There can be no gun control, until WE control the guns...


We were taken from Africa, guns to our heads
And it's because of HIS guns, many of our ancestors are dead
Who was going to every country fighting battles and wars
The Civil War, World Wars I & II, the Persian Gulf War...
Was it you ? Was it me ?


DIARY OF A BLACK MAN....

And even if it was, who controls the guns in the military ?

*CAPOW !!! BANG, BANG !!!*
*SHOOT 'EM UP, RAT-A-TAT-TAT,*
*KAK-KAK-KAK-KAK-KAK !!!*

You know, like i know , for cover we should all run
For, the can be no gun control, Until WE control the guns

In the hood you got kids runnin' all around
With AK's, 9's, 22's, 44's and 357's, 'cause they're down
But who got 'em to the hood ?
Who shipped, who drove ,who stole ,who sold...
All the guns to the hood in the first place ?
Taking About some damn gun control....

*Drive-bys...*
*CAPOW !!! BANG, BANG !!!*
*SHOOT 'EM UP, RAT-A-TAT-TAT,*
*KAK-KAK-KAK-KAK-KAK !!!*

Even Stevie Wonder can see it,
yet it bothers so many others none
There can be no gun control, sistahs and brothas
Until WE control the guns

This new generation got so much energy
So much hostility, that they all want to fight
It's not a bad thing though, understand
It just must be channeled right

Our children must be taught how to clean a gun
And properly shoot a gun
Taught knowledge of self and who the REAL enemy is
And not to pull it or use it on just anyone

They must be taught to love our people
Meaning EVERY sistah and brotha
*WHAT GENOCIDE IS , WHO GENOCIDE IS KILLING*

DIARY OF A BLACK MAN....

And why not to use guns on one another

Cause we've got to keep the spirit alive
In our people, so the battle can be won
For, there can be no gun control
Until WE control the guns...

Who's makin' , shakin', movin ',creatin', exterminatin', inventin' and deliberately pollutin'
The hood with all the guns that we be shootin '?

And some body talkin' about some gun control
To protect who from who ?    Who ARE the dangerous ones ?
There can be no gun control, until somebody else
Somebody like us...       Until somebody other than
The WHITE  man, controls the guns...

CAPOW !!! BANG, BANG !!!
SHOOT 'EM UP, RAT-A-TAT-TAT,KAK-KAK-KAK.... GOT 'EM !!!

DIARY OF A BLACK MAN....

# BROTHA 2 BROTHA

Brotha 2 brotha 2 brotha 2 brotha
It's time we truly take the time
To love one another

Somebody's got a plan, an agenda, a plot
To make sure we kill each other, and always have not

We used to be sold
Upon the auction block
Now we're killing each other
With nines and glocks

Somebody's got us fighting each other
So we can't see
Who's deceiving us
And who's the real enemy

I remember long ago
When we laid side by side
In the bottom of slave ships
Shackled, chained and tied

Though we spoke different languages
And were from different tribes
We knew why we were captured
And who we were captured by

We knew we had to squash our differences
And thick collectively
For, the slave master was no joke
And wasn't gonna set us free

Yes, some were in the field
And some were in the house
But were all of us still not slaves
And equally ordered about?

And was it not obvious
Whether we liked it or not
The house maintenance was just as important

DIARY OF A BLACK MAN....

As the masta's crops ?

And if the brothas plowing and digging
All escaped or were killed
Back the "House Niggahs" would go
Straight to the fields


No matter in what position we might be
We were still just laborers
And nothing more, you see

And now over 400 years later
It's still the same circumstance
We're still divided and conquered
It's just more advanced

More complex is our plight
And much more complicated
Because now were more submissive
For, were more self-hated

So, BROTHA 2 BROTHA
Let me break it down
You know as well as I
The slave master's children don't want us around

And what better way to annihilate us
Than to control our very thoughts
Leading us to act out THEIR fantasies
Through what was subliminally taught

Division through religion
Separation through education
Through class, gender and sexual preference
They fragment the BLAK nation

So what are we gonna do ?
Let them place me against you ?
Are we gonna let them make us out to be
A bunch of African fools ?

Are we going to be their political "Ponnochio's"
As our people get subdued ?

DIARY OF A BLACK MAN....

Or are we going to tell them that no longer
Will we be their trained tools ?

Tell me , will we finally put an end to this
By standing as one
And if necessary, pulling and pointing
In the right direction, our guns ?

**BROTHA 2 BROTHA**
Let's quit the bickering
And all in all, stand tall
So we can finally end this madness
And watch the WHITE man fall !!!

DIARY OF A BLACK MAN....

# Hypocrite or Radical ?

Hypocrite or radical…. which shall I be ?
Shall I stand and look at hypocrisy or fight to get free ?
Am I to accept Christianity and "Uncle Toms" who say
"Jesus is the answer…trust in the Lord…for, that's the only way" ?

After reviewing history, looking back when we were slaves
The slave master planted this religion
and this thought of being "saved"
African people were always spiritual and deeply into God
But we were also rebellious like the Maroons, until Christianity was taught

Back in the motherland, it was the supernatural and mystery
Medicine men, so-called "Witchcraft" and "Voo-Doo" or JuJu
That was practiced by we
But nowadays "Uncle Toms" know as priests
Give sermons and wave their hands
Exclaiming these things are of the devil
just as does the white man…

DIARY OF A BLACK MAN….

They couldn't understand our powers, our righ-
teousness, our love
Our connection, our knowledge and our talents,
given from up above
So they found a way, in the slave days, to make us
passive, yes they did
They taught us THEIR religion, and in turn, we
taught it to our kids
They took it, made different variations, and sever-
al different sects
Different congregations and names, based on the
same text

So this is why I say to my people... is it hypocrisy ?
Or are you still the Africans that you used to be ?
Me ?  I'll never be tainted, my soul won't be
painted
Even if it means HELL
I'm true to my heritage, culture and ancestors
So like a radical....
## I REBEL !!!

DIARY OF A BLACK MAN....

# SEXPERIENCE

Carol, a strong, black queen
Had been independent since the age 16
Met a brotha, like no otha, at a club one night
Who was just her type...

Getting to know, ya know
On the phone they would flow
Workin' hard and oh, my God
Wanted to lay low and take it slow...

But "bro" was so interested
And must've confessed it
A million times, spent a million dimes
Saying "oh please sweetie, won't you be mine ?"
And not just for Valentine's...

So then one day, a Sunday
At her pad, on a pillow they lay
Gettin' buzzed by a good bottle of wine
When next thing you know...TADOW !!!
He was in the behind...

Starting with a kiss, then a lick
Then an eventual stick
A "flick of the Bic", hard, fast, slow, quick

A climax, then a relax, laying on their backs
To a mellow sax, but these be the facts...

Carol practiced safe sex and broke her neck
Not to ever get caught slippin'
While her mate was known for "Honey Dippin"
And even stepped in her house drippin'...
So he, who not only went bareback all the time
When messin' with girls he thought were fine
Also had a fetish for men
That he's sometimes stick it in...

Damn... H.I.V, A-I-D'S, some kind of disease
Brought Carol down to her knees
All because hot and bothered, one time
She didn't have protection, for her mate's erection...

And "bro", he talked a good game
Lame, dumb-brain, about a thousand he slain
Before full blown it became...

So sistahs, ladies, all you fly hotties with thick bodies
Going out and having one night stands
And bringing it home from anotha man, to your brotha man
Who has cheated also
Watch as this disease begins to grow and grow
And next thing you know

Everybody's on death row...

When the solution's abstinence
Which makes perfect since
If you don't want your good health to be a past tense..

When stimulated, since educated
The best way to stay uninfected, is by having masturbated
Cause the tail, on a snail
Or a snake, for heaven's sake
A fly female, tough as nails
Will surely be your demise, if you don't recognize
Those who screw bareback...DIE !!!

So once again to my sistahs, trustin' mistahs
Suckin' on their "peter pissahs"
You better watch your mouth
Cause though they may be fine
They could be gay or "bi" no lie
Or just a mack, a playa, or whatever

Givin' you a lil' somethin' somethin' that'll take you out
Or leave a scar on your health forever...

DIARY OF A BLACK MAN....

# BOTTLE OF WINE

Last night I sat down with a bottle of wine
And tried to clear my mind, and what did I find ?
I found brothas and sistahs all shades of brown in my head
Most of them brain dead...

I found my people who everyday, be lookin' the other way
Tryin' to get paid and laid
But mostly just getting cheated, defeated and mistreated
I found indigenous brothas and othas
Being self-hated, miseducated and manipulated

Then I said Damn...Is it the wine ?
That is making me NOT see blind ?
Is it because, I caught a buzz
That I finally see what is and what was ?

Jesus drank wine, if there was such a man
Oops!!!  My mind might be going too deep, for my peoples asleep
When I say they ignore us...and Isis, Osirus and Horus
Or Heru, that'll help you see through
All the bull shit that the psuedo-Semites
And Romans have used to  mislead you

And I trip off how Mexicans, Guatemalans and even some Cubans
Relate and even sometimes claim Spain
Are they dead in the brain or just plain insane ?
When they take on Catholism without knowing
They should be growing, but instead they're blowing
All the great spiritual things our ancestors left

DIARY OF A BLACK MAN....

That are so in-depth, they should be kept...

So many thoughts flew and fly, through my 3rd eye
I want to cry....Cause people of color slowly die
As I sipped and tripped, I instantly knew
I'd never remember these thoughts when my buzz was through
So I sat down and wrote THIS, which was on my mind
And thought Damn...ain't nothing like a good bottle of wine..

DIARY OF A BLACK MAN....

# WATCH

*Watch us struggle and make ends meet*
*Watch us take mere scraps and make a meal to eat*

*Watch us wear clothing all tattered and torn*
*And just like magic, watch as a new style is born*

*Watch us stumble over a new language*
*Perfecting it, after dissecting it, through dialecting it*

*Watch us take spirituality to a whole new, yet very old level*
*Defying your beliefs, your expectations, your ideologies*
*Your psuedo-mythologies...*

*Watch us stare with bare feet, stripped of everything but our skin*
*As you physically separate the African from Africa*
*But can never take the Africa from within...*

*Watch us relearn what we already knew*
*By culture and by nature*
*Watch as we expose your plots and lies*
*As you claim that we just hate you*

*Watch as we never, ever dog our people...*
*Watch as we give more love than ever*
*To our children, grandparents, women and men*
*Assuring and reassuring, that we the people*
*Will definitely rise again...*

*Watch as we take your laws, government systems and military bases*
*Learn them, master them and turn them inside out*
*Exploding like bombs in your faces...*

*Watch as we return to being*
*The 3 million year old creators of the world*

DIARY OF A BLACK MAN....

*As your stomach gets nauseated and your head swirls...*

*Even on the bottom, in the sewers, the gutters, jail cells and gutters*
*Our survival instincts and immune systems are still "top notch"*
*And we be creating, composing, inventing and making things happen*
*Just as we did in the beginning, and...WE WILL SURVIVE....*

# *JUST WATCH !!!*

DIARY OF A BLACK MAN....

# FAREWELL...

You know, WHITE strategies to destroy people of color, are really, really a trip
I remember when "Cracka's" used to be cowboys and soldiers, with guns upon their hips

Nowadays it's about the system itself, and most of them don't have to do a thing
For, the system of white supremacy works by itself, and to the lower levels, it keeps non-whites chained

It kills us daily through mental slavery, divided and conquered and all on welfare
Not to mention what happens to a people purposely contaminated, then denied adequate health care...

Don't you know it's all systematic and part of the ultimate plan
Premeditated genocide through denial of medical benefits
Conceived and concocted by the WHITE man

The "Indians " know what I'm talking about, that syphilis really did them in Hell, A common cold or anything else, can become deadly without medicine...

Asthma, glaucoma, heart attacks due to stress or whatever else one may get
All can be disastrous when health care is a luxury, and a whole group of people can't afford it

If you notice what kills people of color, especially BLAKS in the U.S.A.
It's minor problems that have turned major because routine check-up bills they can't pay

And AIDS, the germ warfare released, so people of color would decease
Came from the beast, but wasn't on a leash
And now AIDS has taken them too..
For, it sees no color, so now what should one do ?

But there's a cure, I'm sure, yet alot of us die faster

DIARY OF A BLACK MAN....

And why? Because we can't afford the medicines
The prescriptions to stop the pain within..

So systematically it's spreading, watch it spread
As impoverished people still deal with stress through drug use
Or having sex in the bed...

Damn... no health care, no health care
Cause nobody's caring about their health
We're on welfare, health care...care about your health
Care about yourself...

We must petition march, rebel, riot and vote
Fight, steal, kill or grab Uncle Sam by the throat !!!

We must do something, because no health care, is like no welfare...
It's like no caring about humanity's welfare
Which is like having no one left
Which all adds up to one big backwards welfare
And you know what that is ?

# FAREWELL !!!

DIARY OF A BLACK MAN....

# THE SOUL THAT NEVER WAS

In a city, in a state, not often heard of
Portland, Oregon, there lies a sistah
With a different kind of love...

Growing up in a city, where what was pretty
In most men's eyes, was BLUE eyes, blond hair
And skin that was "fair"
She found no brothas interested in her there...

So, needing attention, need I mention
Who gave it to her and offered to "do" her
That wanna be cool, wanna be down
But skin nowhere near brown
Vanilla Ice, wanting a slice,
Marky Mark, fiending for the dark
Third Base, pale face
Otha than a brotha, dirty motha
Who with a BLAK girl on his arm
Felt he was that much closer to the race
He desired to be a part of...

The blind leading the blinded, one might suggest
And even I must confess
Brothas dating "othas' sure thought they were blessed...

So, one after another she would date,
Hoping one could truly relate
But she always found something missing
Even though her ass, cave-boy was constantly kissing
For that extra special feeling she was wishing...
But, no luck, FUCK, she was kinda stuck
And mom wasn't exactly afrocentric
Hell, she didn't mind
Her daughter dating another kind

DIARY OF A BLACK MAN....

And being straight-up blind...

School didn't teach her nothing about African-American history
Except that same ol' Harriet Tubman, Martin Luther King
Used to be slaves crap
And even the cave-boys had mastered that,,,


So all through high-school, it was tough
Trying to find herself
While she was constantly scrutinized
By everybody else
Every man she ever dated, only related
To her sexual, not intellectual, part
Played with her mind and broke her heart...

But strong inside, though not knowing why, she was
Even when abused by the slave master
Who would dog his own lilly-white women
But would degrade her even faster
Leaving no one left except the feminist
Who caught wind of this
And recruited, saluted, diluted and then polluted
This sistah with homosexual, male-hating thoughts
Secretly disguised and encoded in feminist rhetoric
How pathetic...

This sistah who was born NOT to know
You must become African WITHIN America at home
Because mom didn't teach her, or care to reach her
Has now become a dike,,,
And her own brotha
She has never even had a desire to like...

As she vacations to northern "calli"
With a WHITE hippie named Sally

DIARY OF A BLACK MAN....

**And is suddenly involved in Gay Rights' rallies ?**

**It's quite a shame how middle-class blacks
Raise their children and never think about building
Strong African images in their hearts and brains
To break the European chains and strains
Placed upon us while attending white schools
Our African children end up fools
Deceived by the false interpretation
Of the history of this nation
And sistahs like this one, get turned out or fall prey
To WHITE boys or those gay
While trying to find out who she really is
But never doing so because...
She like so many others, possesses
The soul that never, ever, really, truly was...**

DIARY OF A BLACK MAN....

# *DEATH BED*

As I lay, looking up at the ceiling
Body and soul slowly parting from one another
One thing should be heard, one thing should be said
Don't let me die in vain, when I decease on my death bed

I do not want a Catholic priest, A Baptist priest
Or ANY priest, to say the least, praying over me...
Don't let anyone put their religious hands on my head
When I die, laying on my death bed

Do not part me out like a broken down car
Giving a limb to him, a lung to her, kidney to them
Do not donate one drop of the blood I have bled
Or remove my heart when it beats no more
Upon my death bed...

I don't want to be buried in a "Negro" cemetery
Nor in the south, north, east or west of America
Do not put me in a casket all fancy, but instead
BURN THESE BONES, when I am still, upon my death bed

I want fire and flame to surround my skin
Melting it away, leaving no memory
Of the trouble it's been
Until only ashes I am, placed in a cup of tin or lead
When just a corpse I am, upon my death bed

Take me to Africa, the jungles, the city, the terrain
The sands ,the mountains, the lakes
Where my soul can be peaceful

Once my body has been shed
Let my ashes blow like leaves
Once I leave my death bed

Home I will be, home, home, home
Where my spirit has meaning, within its comfort zone
Release my remains and forever I shall be
With my people, no more death bed
I am now truly free...

# RIGHT ABOUT NOW

Oh, say can you see ?    As the so-called land of the free
Home of the brave, enters a new decade
I look back on the so-called progress that has been made...

As America, the BEAST itself, claims a new found love
For multiculturalism and ethnic diversity
And the elite upper-class, white trash
Still control coerce, manipulate, dominate, segregate and hate
On a whole 'nother level, like a bunch of devils
Ethnic populations, especially American-Africans
Struggle to survive...

While Affirmative Action, which never gave those oppressed satisfaction
Is now reviewed and unrenewed
Is the little bit of hope that
" There are some good WHITE people out there somewhere, aren't there ?"

Welfare reform, which is really reforming
A home-wrecking, forever economically crippling
Systematic sharecropping, genocidal pill popping,  government system
That unbelievably only costs 3 cents on every dollar
But would've only costed 5 cents to be a useful tool
Is more than just cruel...
As the make-up of the BLAK family means
No money and no food, unless you get rid of your dude
And those are the welfare rules...

So many wonder why brothas and sistahs have attitudes
When lousy educational institutions
And poor quality, run-down high, junior-high and even preschools

DIARY OF A BLACK MAN....

Are given to ethnic populations, so that they are psychologically incapable
Of learning too much that might be useful
People know that environment plays a big part in how much a child grows
THOSE WHITE PEOPLE KNOW !!!
Why do you think they have tutors and computers in theirs
Yet they claim everything is fair ?     Be aware !!!


As unconscious "minorities" struggle to get a piece
Of that American pie
And for us, the well remains forever dry
WHITES just lie, lie and lie
And then turn around and exclaim "All you have to do is try"

Integration is the biggest farce
Yet colonized people of color do their part
To force themselves into neighborhoods and businesses
That  absolutely do not want them
Instead of just staring their own
And building their own homes
Like they did for the pilgrims, when forced
But are too lazy to do for themselves, of course...

WHEN ARE YOU GOING TO WAKE UP ?
Shut the fuck up, with all the cryin', bickerin'
Dodgin', ditchin' and bitchin'
And realize;      WHITES ARE NOT YOUR FRIENDS !!!
They are not sincere
And the only "forty" you're ever going to get
Won't be in acres, but in rat poison in a bottle
Malt liquor beer...

While even WHITE liberals know it's wrong
But won't argue too much, as long as the scales of America
Are tipped in White people's  favor
Cause they love the flavor...


DIARY OF A BLACK MAN....

You best be comin' to the conscious side, to the "colored" side
To the ethnic side, to the BLAK pride side
Like all of your ancestors who've died
'Cause if you don't, you'll never find a solution
Unless you too, turn to REVOLUTION

**CONTROL YOUR OWN DESTINY**
When, where and how?
Stop integratin', matin' relatin'
And start savin', behavin' and sacrificin'

# RIGHT ABOUT...NOW !!!

DIARY OF A BLACK MAN....

# VOICE

I don't think I have an inner-voice
Though someone told me that I had no choice
I did not and I still don't think I have a "writing voice"
Or a certain style when I write
But some other artist told me I had one
And would have one, no matter how hard I fight

My inner-voice is a revolutionary one
My inner voice tells me to go and get a gun
But I hear Toni Morrison, Sonia Sanchez and Maya Angelou
Talk about finding that inner-voice
And me.... I think NOT having one
Or
NOT thinking that I have one
Is a voice within itself

What ? I can't believe it !!!
It's kinda like a painter
Take Picasso, who has no style
Which IS his own style, you know?

I speak how I think, I write how I speak
I think in a dreamy, hazy, kind of dazy, down-to-earth,
Realistic, mystical way...of what could be
And I'm very opinionated

Yet I express it in no particular voice
So, that's my style... Yep, that's me !!!

# LOVED TO DEATH

IMANI, a nice honey,
Had been with her man, since jr.high began
It was all love and fun, until she turned 21
For, that's when the real trouble begun...

Hanging out with her friends, getting hit on by other men
Staying out 'til the club ends, her man thought was a sin
Insecure, I'm sure, he'd abuse her and bruise her
Though her love was pure, he acted way too immature

But, stay with the kid she did, even when he flipped his lid
Why? 'cause with him, she'd already did a 10-year bid
Thinking love for God and praying,
Would stop, her from getting popped
Mentally, physically and emotionally abused
But yo, yo yo...this kid wasn't playin'

So to work she would go, bruises would show
Accidental falls she would claim,
But co-workers were hip to the game
Thinking it was her fault, she tried hard to bring it to a halt
Not taking anything her man said "with a grain of salt"

She changed her style of dress, her hair, but hell, he didn't care
He still beat her and didn't treat her, nowhere near fair
Until one day, sad to say, the beating she took was fatal
Cause low and behold he was able
To pick her up, throw her across the room
And then beat her down with one of the legs from the kitchen table

So my sistahs, my sistahs, let this be a lesson
If you're guessin' from a man you've got to take this shit
Every man ain't a man, so understand
You ain't his queen, if in your relationship, you be gettin' hit

Domestic violence is worse when there's silence
And you allow the pain and suffering to continue

DIARY OF A BLACK MAN....

*It'll only get worse, and in the end you might not get hurt*
*It may be your life that you somehow lose...*

*So choose to speak out*
*Against domestic violence, know what I'm talking about ?*

# WHEN?

As I sit by and watch the world become more and more wicked
I think about God and say... WHEN ?
As African people continue to feel the ongoing, never-ending
Legacy of oppression, I think to myself... WHEN ?

When will so many engaged in substance abuse realize it's all a plan
To keep them in a vulnerable, helpless state ?
When will they realize they need to stand up and be the strong , proud
Africans that their ancestors used to and they too have to power to be...WHEN ?

When will Africans in America realize we are divided and therefore conquered
And  unity amongst African peoples ALL over,
And then eventually, ALL people of color, is the only path  to true freedom
And control of the lands once preserved, respected, worshipped and inhabited
By our ancestors and other indigenous peoples'... if not now  WHEN ?

When will South Africans realize democracy is only a step
And as long as even (1 ) WHITE  lives within the country
BLAKS will never control the diamond industry or other exported resources
And therefore, will NEVER control South Africa, meaning  they will never
Truly become free ?

When will South Africans realize REVOLUTION and chasing the whites out
Is the ONLY logical solution and guarantee of a better country...
When will they see this... If not now  WHEN ?

When will ALL people of color stop falling for the tricks, traps, plots and plans
Of the WHITE races ?
When will they stand up and  stand together realizing that whether WHITES call
Themselves Christians, Muslims, Mormons, Jews, Rastas, Democrats or Liberals
They are out to exploit those of color and have been since their arrival to the
New world, Asia, South America, AFRICA, and the Caribbean...
When will people of color stand up and end this systematic annihilation of the
Natural resources, the environment, nature itself and also the animals... WHEN ?

When will people of color finally say  "Enough is Enough !!!"... WHEN ?

When will the People of color in America realize that all the voting in the world
Will not change the status quo;  and there is no such of a thing as

DIARY OF A BLACK MAN....

A "good WHITE president", for, they all come from the same, elite, upper-class And
:
THEY ARE ALL WHITE !!!    WHEN ?

When will people of color realize they are the majority NOT the minority
And unity will completely destroy this wicked system...WHEN ?

When will all this happen...WHEN ?

Our children are being born into a world full of sacrifice
We could make sure they receive all that they deserve... so tell me WHEN?
We have waited, as the clock ticks
And I look out my window and stare into the sky
I ask ...WHEN ?

WHEN WILL GOD, if there is a God, put an end to all this wickedness....
Please tell me...
# WHEN ?

DIARY OF A BLACK MAN....

# HOLLYWOOD

Checkered table cloths are like racing flags to me
Hard plastic chairs, make-up and hair
Cheaply made food, caterers that are rude
Why? Cause I need to pay my bills dude

A million and one stories of ambition
Disappointment, accomplishments and secret missions
Old worn out faces, staring to say
"A line, a line for me today ?"

Back stabbin', rat poisonin', in this rat race
Smug, smerky quivers, stressed looks, a poker face
Desperation, competition, auditions, cheap sex for success
Hollywood has wicked ways...

Break you down they will, if they can
Anything some will do, for a little cash in hand
Glamour, fame, fortune and a name
Superficial things, after death are all the same

They eat away, grab and puncture your soul
They persist and if you resist
With one kiss, your on the black list

## Welcome to HOLLYWOOD...

# B-CONSCIOUS

## OF

# D-KNOWLEDGE

You, me and we can always
kick, pull, hold, keep and drop... *D-KNOWLEDGE*
But I, you and they don't always..B-CONSCIOUS

I, you and we can go to school, to college campuses
Talk to people on the street, forever hear speakers
And learn... *D-KNOWLEDGE*
But that does not mean that you, me and we will:
      B-CONSCIOUS

So many people like Clarence Thomas, Colin Powell, Bryant Gumble, Byron Allen and Jesse Jackson have...
      *D-KNOWLEDGE*
But not all of them or ANY of them, are or ever will...
      B-CONSCIOUS

So remember this...
It does not always take *D-KNOWLEDGE* to B-CONSCIOUS
Sometimes *D-KNOWLEDGE* you gain

DIARY OF A BLACK MAN....

May mess up your brain...

But even some of the illiterate, due to their sights, sounds
Their immediate surroundings, environment
And day to day interactions, B, like you B, like I B, like we B
And even the enemy B... they...    B-CONSCIOUS

SO DON'T WORRY ABOUT   *D-KNOWLEDGE*
BUT TRY YOUR HARDEST EVERYDAY TO Be AND STAY
LIKE THOSE WHO TRULY    B-CONSCIOUS

DIARY OF A BLACK MAN....

# JUICED

A lemon... watch this land make a lemon into an orange
Watch this orange drop a seed and grow an orange tree
Watch this orange tree bear much fruit...

A lime... watch a lime get turned into an apple by an orange
Watch the orange and the apple create an apple tree
Watch the apple tree bear fruits of strange flavors
Watch the apple get bored with the orange...

The apple now likes pears
Watch the affair between the apple and the pear
They are unaware, but they are about to get juiced
By the orange...

Watch as the apple gets turned into applesauce
And the pear gets diced
And the orange...
The orange gets taken to the supermarket
He's unaware, but now HE'S about to get juiced...

Watch as the orange gets put in the juicer
By the supermarket clerk
Round and round the orange goes,
Getting squeezed for all his seeds, but he has a tough skin...
So as the juicer peels and peels slowly,
Slowly but surely the orange get's liquefied... JUICED

Watch as the orange becomes juice
The apple that used to be a lime, is now sauce
And all have lost...

The pear that didn't have a care

DIARY OF A BLACK MAN....

Is now diced and cannot drop a seed
For a tree to bear any fruit...

The orange, once a lemon, is now O.J. and gets juiced...
What a waste...
The applesauce spoils, the diced pear dries up
And the juice evaporates...

DIARY OF A BLACK MAN....

# ABORTED

Spirits of ancestors long gone, try to live on
Martyrs have tried to come back, only to be attacked
Past leaders, great men and women of history have tried
To come back as infants, and undelivered have died
Mighty people that historians in the past recorded
Were coming back to save us, and instantly got aborted

Sometimes I think of Jesus, and if indeed
He was making a "second coming", the entrance he'd need
And I realize he'd be born again, to another woman REAL strong
But then I think about abortions, And I realize why he's taking so long

Jesus, Moses, ALL the prophets, plus a million more
Have probably been trying to come back, but getting stopped at the door
Dying a million deaths, while feeling all nice and snug
Ready to be born again, until somebody pulled the plug

Future presidents and saviors who could end our misery
Are more than likely conceived everyday, only to be put to sleep
So many artists, teachers and inventors, who would've given us a better life
See light and then get it put out, with the snip, snip of a doctor's knife

What a thought..All these bad things in the world, in each individual nation
Might not exist, if pregnant mothers weren't killing whole generations
But I guess that's one's own choice
For, one can't hear the itty, bitty voice
Of little ones of the present and the past
Who are given life, but then lose it, all too fast

People should B-CONSCIOUS of all the spirits and souls
Returning to be rejected, extinguished or controlled
For, the creator NEVER gives you more than you can handle
So why not take a chance ?

DIARY OF A BLACK MAN....

There's no telling who or what you will give birth to
And whose life or lives that will enhance...

# DYING

BLAK people are dying...
In the jails, on the streets, in the hospitals
In the jungles of Africa
We are dying...

We are dying from alcohol poisoning
drug abuse, crack, caffeine, tobacco
And bad nutrition...

Not to mention Birth controlled, coat hanger
Prescribed abortions and Planned parenthood clinics
We are dying...

I am dying...you are dying...blaks are dying
From the poor health care
and systematic annihilation diseases...
We are dying...

They have a million and one ways to kill us
And come up with a thousand new ways each year
They've even taught us how to kill ourselves
So, We are killing ourselves...

I am dying...you are dying
you are killing me...I am killing you
You are killing you...and i am killing me too

They are killing us...everybody is killing us

I want to live...don't you want to live ?
stop killing us...let's stop killing us
Stop the killing... and by any means necessary
Let's live...

# a "g" thang

When I think of a "G", what do I see ?
First off a Gangstah living unconsciously
A Genocidal General, Galloping on the city streets
Greedy for Green, with a Gun, Geared to Give Grief

On the term "O.G.", what does the "G" really stand for ?
A Grave digger with Gusto and "Grass" Galore
Glorifying Gangs like a Ghastly Ghost in this nation
A Ghetto Germ, A Gladiator, Gobbling up this Generation

A "G" could be a Genius or a Guardian
A Guru even, for those who represent the Genuine
But instead a "G" is a Greasy Goon...
A Goof ball who Guzzles Gin
A Gloomy, Grouchy, Grafitti-writing Giant

## Who's Great for the Government

A "G", what is a "G" to me?
Well, to make it simple and plain
To Grab some Grammar and Graciously Grade one
This word is what hits my brain:

# GARBAGE !!!

DIARY OF A BLACK MAN....

# SLAVE THREADS

*Watching a show, a talk show*
*About some clothing designers, made me say*
*"YO... WHAT'S UP WITH US, BRO?"*

*Tommy Hillfigure*
*Openly said he don't make his clothes*
*For no "hip-hop" niggahs*
*Ralph Lauren*
*Stated: "When I design, it ain't for Blak men..."*

*"I don't owe the African-American community a thing.."*
*Exclaimed the boot company TIMBERLAND*
*Nike, Adidas, Puma, La Gear and Fila*
*Haven't any BLAKS on their boards of directors*
*And swear up and down they don't need us*

*Yet, tennis shoe commercials are full of*
*Exploited basketball players, catchy slogan sayers*
*Pawns of the game, out to get paid*
*While BLAKS get falsely portrayed and then slayed*
*Making one ask "Are BLAKS just afraid?"*

*Not to buy any products or goods*
*That exploit our community and neighborhoods*
*Are they too damn blind to see*
*That wearin' devils' bull shit threads*
*Make us look stupider than stupid, foolish as hell*
*And deader than dead*

*Even my sistahs be runnin' out and buyin that Donna Karan*
*Who don't be carin', about what "Aunt Jemimas be wearin'"*
*And Liz Claiborne, who with scorn*
*Told the world that on BLAK women*
*Her clothes weren't meant to be worn*

*So what's up? What's wrong brothas and sistahs?*
*Are you that asleep? Or afraid of lookin' cheap?*
*Is that why we don't manufacture our own garments*
*And earn our own keep?*

DIARY OF A BLACK MAN....

*We need to do somethin', instead of frontin'*
*'Cause wearin' the slave masters plantation outfits*
*To the rest of the world , don't mean nothin'*
*'cept the man, who owns the name on the brand*
*Has the whip in his hand*
*Keeping you a slave who behaves...      Now you understand ?*

DIARY OF A BLACK MAN....

# SOMETHING

*I must make something out of nothing*
*I must create a way to deal with this beast*
*I must let my tears flow like raindrops*
*Running through the streets*
*I must be and say what I am...*

*I must make something out of nothing*
*I just want to scream and shout and throw things*
*And go into a frenzy...*
*I wonder if GOD can hear us down here ?*
*"We're oppressed!!! Help us damn it !!!"*

*I must make something out of nothing*
*Like ancestors given poor living quarters*
*A new language, a new religion and pork fat*
*Plus other scraps not good for your health...*
*With these things we created our own paradise*
*Our own lingo, slang and dialect,*
*Our own spirituality filled with soul*
*And our own cuisine known as soul food*
*Hell, we created our own culture*
*Out of nothing...*

*I must make something out of nothing*
*If I don't, I'll end up killing myself*
*Or attempting to kill everybody I see as an oppressor*
*And in the process, I'll probably end up killing myself too*

*So i take my pen, and jot down*
*These symbols called letters*
*That leave an impression on the souls*
*Of a many men... long after I'm gone*
*Making minds that once saw nothing*
*Now see and feel something...*

*I feel nothing but pain, hurt, distrust and sometimes fear*
*For this pseudo land of the free, home of the slave*
*In which they gave us for free, nothing...*

*And with that, I make, I create*

DIARY OF A BLACK MAN....

*Images on paper and in the ears of my people*
*I leave stains upon their brains*
*Motivating them to action*
*Now ain't that something ?*
*Out of nothing...*

DIARY OF A BLACK MAN....

# ESCAPE

Trapped, confused
Lost in a world I did not create
My daily tasks grow, my every effort is put forth
To help me successfully escape...

I spend nights dreaming, spacing out
Distant from my head resting place
With tears kissing my pillow, wonder I do
How I can deal with the anxiety
Staring me in the face

Words unrhythmically flowing, but showing
I can't help but write to express my pain
Escaping doesn't mean I have to leave
The habitat I'm accustomed to
It just means I have to prevent myself
From going insane

How can I leave the knowledge, consciousness and culture
I've learned in the past, behind ?
It's hard as hell to escape
When the jail cell is locked in my mind

My queen of the universe, for whom I thirst
Is my only vehicle to get away, some days
When I crumble like a cookie in her arms
Escape we try through making love
And if one of us cracks, the other isn't alarmed

I comb the earth, I probe my brain
And only with my scribbler, letters, vowels, syllables
Synonyms, verbs, pronouns, adjectives, cliche's
Phrases and verses of emotions

DIARY OF A BLACK MAN....

Do I break those mental, physical, emotional, social
And political chains...

I HAVE ESCAPED

# LAZINESS

Lazy and tired I am
Unfulfilled with my life
**Heart~break misery, lack of true emotion**
Lack of forgiveness for wrong doings

Helplessness, disappointment
**Knowing not how to cure my loneliness**
I desperately search for clues
Where are you at ?

**Where do I find my niche' ?**
Myself ?
I'm still looking...

**Lies, lies, lies... all I hear are lies**
About my path, about my future
My potential...

**Afraid I am, I'll wake up middle aged**
Elderly, over~the~hill, all beat~up
With nothing but my procrastination
**Talents unused, and why ?**
I dream, I dream

But eventually I got to get up and quit being lazy...

# BROTHERHOOD

Just chillin',
bondin',
communicatin',
understandin'
Laughin',
cryin',
disageein',
dependin',
trustin',
plannin'
BROTHERHOOD

Exceptin',
growin',
buildin',
teachin',
helpin',
lovin'
Lovin' my brothas,
lovin' the fact that we have
BROTHERHOOD

Listenin',
explainin',
respectin',
trippin'
Enjoyin',
celebratin',
explorin',
definin'
BROTHERHOOD

Recognizin',
supplyin',
borrowin',
reachin',
savin'
Upliftin',
unifyin',
cooperatin'
in the name of
BROTHERHOOD

Brotherhood is our number one asset and strength

DIARY OF A BLACK MAN....

And to protect it, we must be willing to go to all lengths

# THE ARENA

*Conceived, brought forth, from a mother's womb*
*Born to intake knowledge, observe and consume*
*Prepared to go forth, obtain and posses*
*Morals, virtues and traditions, once put to rest*

*Resurrect the souls of ancestors long gone*
*To insure that the movement will live on*
*Once strong and wise, forward I go*
*Into the arena to challenge my foes*

*This dreadful place where we all must fight*
*Usually alone, but occasionally we unite*
*So often jumping out the ring, because we can't cope*
*Our knowledge is our boxing gloves and the laws are the ropes*

*Fighting the arch enemy, who doesn't give a damn*
*The three-time, heavyweight champion of the world...*
*The devil himself...    Uncle Sam*
*As the bell rings, my heart pounds and round one begins*
*Alone in the battle without my circle of friends*

*Blow after blow is thrown, as I duck, dodge but can't hide*
*Laying down in the ring isn't even an option*
*For, inside lies too much pride...*
*So, swing after swing I anticipate, hoping to throw an uppercut*
*However eventually a glove hits me, knocking me down on my butt*

*"Get up, get up" I tell myself, before my legs have time to react*
*Surviving in the ring is the name of the game*
*And if you're lucky , you'll get to swing back*
*But for most, one blow leads to another, another and still another*
*Then before one knows it they're knocked out*
*Or with punches smothered*
*Some say with stamina and concentration*
*One can indeed become the victor*
*Even though their opponent in the ring, may be ten times bigger...*
*Others say if one uses the psychological approach*
*You can win this and all bouts without even a coach*

*But most people making these statements haven't a clue*
*How to actually fight the fight or what the hell they would do*
*For, most spectators love to watch, and even occasionally place a bet*
*Critical of the ones in the ring, as outside the arena they sit*

*Shit, my mother, father and ancestors fought the fight in this ring*
*Most of the lost, some of them had draws, but not one won a thing*
*So for them especially, I put on my gloves in my early years*

DIARY OF A BLACK MAN....

And make the arena my permanent home, and fighting my lifetime career

Knowing even though I break a sweat, everyday of my life
Until everybody decides to jump in the ring
There will be no end to this fight...
For, there's too much power behind the champ
And alone, he'll surely cream ya
But despite this fact, where I'll be at
Until death, is fighting for freedom in the arena

DIARY OF A BLACK MAN....

# NOTEBOOKS

Full of dreams
Scribbled on are sheets
Bound together by emotion and rubber
But never quite complete

Sometimes I wonder
What will I do when I finish ?
Before my interrupted fantasies
Like  reflections in a pond, diminish

I sometimes feel my writings
Are just useless notes
My voice sometimes comes out hoarse
Like somebody has me by the throat

But devote my time,I still do
To perfecting my craft
Knowing in the sea of unrighteousness
For someone, I shall provide a raft

No oars will be needed
As my style and wording will tell
All that is unspoken by many
Symbolizing a cultural sail

Taking on some expeditions
To heaven and/or hell
In the end my spirit and soul
Will forever prevail

DIARY OF A BLACK MAN....

This is why I never throw anything out
To be read or stolen by crooks
So when you enter my humble, dwelling spot
You'll see tons and tons of unfinished notebooks...

DIARY OF A BLACK MAN....

# PENNIES FROM HEAVEN

*Sometimes I look around and say to myself
"Thank God I've been dropped on this earth
The little bit I do to save this planet each day
Tells the creator exactly how much I'm worth*

*I feel we are all pennies from heaven
Put on the earth to amount to something
Banned together in large groups, we are powerful
Even alone, we are more than mere nothings*

*Copper-coated, caramel, dark-brown and bronze too
We make nickels dimes, quarters and dollars
We together, accomplish so, so much
And in the world trade market we go farther*

*For, we are the beginning and without us
All that is valuable would be gone
One plus one equals two, plus two equals four
Plus one more equals five and so on*

*I feel pennies from heaven we are
Dropped from the heavens above
Put on this earth to amount to something
To make a difference with the value of our love*

# TRICKERY

Trick me ?  you think you can
But  humor me only, you don't under-
stand...

Kill me ?  Attempt you do, in all ways
But only anger me, you've done And
cease to amaze

Every breathing creature, Plant and
earthly form
Manipulate, control, capture And kill is
your norm

Make things even, shall we surely, for
what is odd
So clever you think you are, But still can-
not fool God

The creator is watching, taking accurate
notes

DIARY OF A BLACK MAN....

Giving one the power To stay afloat

Endure and survive in your cold days, The creator provides the coat
Which warms and enables those loyal, To grab you by the throat

We are the sorcerers Who are magically gifted
And above you rudimentary trickery, We shall be lifted

By the spirit, by ourselves, Through the universal power
Leaving your pranks, with only yourself to devour

# no more tricks

## LATINO RELATIONS

Man, I trip off BLAK and Latino relations...
All the indigenous brothas are trying to do is survive...
Aren't you ?      Wouldn't you ?

Burrito trucks fill their barrios; swap meets
Selling everything on their neighborhood streets
Trying to make a buck, down on their luck
And in second-class citizenship stuck... Just like us

Forever seeking a way, to get paid
But without too much pride inside
To take any job right away
Plumbers, gardeners, housekeepers, maids and janitors too
Yo, Yo, Yo, they gots to do, what they gots to do
What about me and you ?

They sell dope, smoke and drink when they can't cope
And you think they're free from genocide and self-hate ?   Nope ...
Speaking a new language, Spainish AND  English...Damn, that's two !!!
Because just like so many, they too
Have had the oppressor cut away their roots

But they're still survivin', strivin', trying to live and even dyin'
With other people of color voting for proposition !87
Is that truly what will make the so-called land of the free, heaven ?
187...just like the police code
187...death, killing... are we in that mode ?
If so, I think you and me know who and where
To begin, to start to make everything fair
Because our indigenous brothas are just trying to survive...
Aren't you ?      Wouldn't you ?

Selling produce on the street corners and freeways

Hell, BLAK folks wouldn't do that shit noways
Talking about we're getting underbidded and undercut...So what !!!
Quit pimpin' welfare and get off your butts
We could pool our resources, produce our own goods
Have soul food trucks in our hoods...If we tried


Divided and conquered we are, and thus far
It looks like Mr, colonizer has won
But the battle has really just begun
We must understand about the Mexican
Who is often times called Latino, but is really Indian
This is THEIR land...
So before you can even attempt to get mad
Just remember they lost all they had
And you don't think they feel bad ?

Taking the lowest of low jobs,
Of wages getting basically robbed
While the government doesn't mind
And you don't truly mind either, don't lie !!!
Or would you rather see prices on everything, shoot up sky high ?

So B-CONSCIOUS and B-real,
B careful of the enemy, yet still
Don't let your guard down, cause everybody brown ain't down
And some of them don't want you around...
But they're just trying to survive... aren't you ? Wouldn't you ?

This is why I say to you, from our indigenous brothas, we could learn
How not to waste money we earn, so we too won't get burned
Unite ...teach and reach all peoples of color
So we can stop being pitted against one another
And realize the enemy is the colonizer
Not your indigenous red, yellow, brown or BLAK brotha
After all, they're just trying to survive
In this wicked system of oppression....Aren't you ?


DIARY OF A BLACK MAN....

# hip-hop

HIp-hOP. CONfusion

ILLUSIONS OF FreedOM EXPLOitatION ... Minimal monetary gratifications ... for cOntributions, **Lack of solutions Ever growing problems...** *Not enough knowledge to go around ?*
      **Trapped**
  LOST
CHAINED TO THIS WORLD OF POVERTY AND SELFISHNESs
**Naive,** blinded, *mislead*, **manipulated**
   Controlled and coerced into genocidal practices
Distressed, FRUSTRATED *DESPERATE*
    HUNGRY
*CRIMINAL-MINDED POPULATION* OUT OF SURVIVAL INSTINCTS
Drinking, shooting-up, snortin' **blazin' and blazin', Slowly but surely** dyin'

DIARY OF A BLACK MAN....

**Mothers, oh mothers,** *nursing* rearing,
**teaching**
*training,* **laughing,** but mostly *cryin'*
Disrespectin', **neglectin'** usin', *abusin'*, dissin', trippin', **braggin'** boastin'
*And forever fighting for a spot on top*

*Ego trippin',* slippin' dippin', *pimpin',* playin' rhyme sayin'
**Tryin' to be hard,**
Acting unaffected, protected, keeping up one's guard
Because really insecure, unsure and **immature**
WITH NO DIRECTION is my people's in *HIP-HOP*

DIARY OF A BLACK MAN....

# DESIRE

I have the desire to be all that my ancestors used to be.

I want to be a mathematician, knowing all the formulas and equations
For everything in the universe.

I want to be an astrologist, knowing each and every comet, star, planet
And solar system by name...
I want to understand the sun and the moon
And their relationship and effect upon everything.

I want to be a scientist, like those who created and discovered cures
That were natural, herbal and from the earth
Before western man's medicinal attempts...

I want to be an artist, a creator
Like those who created pyramids from sandstone
Pots, tools and temples...

I want to be a pharaoh, I want to be a GOD
Like ISIS, OSIRUS, HERU or HORUS
AMEN, AMEN-RA or the MEDU NETCHER

I want to be wise, for knowledge is power
And with that comes strength.

I want to be able to communicate with African people all over the world.
From Ghana to Ethiopia, Euritrea to Tanzania, Nubia to New England
Canada to Haiti to Harlem to London to Los Angeles...
I want to know THEIR dialects and languages
So we can all speak as one, think as one, and live as one.

The more I desire, the more I realize
My desires are alot closer to reality, than I believe them to be
My desire to be all that I can or have the potential to be
To be all that my ancestors used to be
My ability to learn, to follow to become is easy.
All of my desires are already deep inside of me....

So, I will search within myself and only there will I find
That my desires, dreams, my goals and the things I want to be
I've actually been the whole time...

# ABOUT THE AUTHOR:

# Tony B. Conscious

*Hip-Hop / Funk / Rock / Soul / Spoken Word Artist*

A renaissance man (Harlem Renaissance that is), **TONY B. CONSCIOUS** is the personification of
AFRICAN-AMERICAN culture.

He is (amongst other things) A B-BOY, BEATBOX, EMCEE, GRAFFITI/VISUAL ARTIST (known as "THE GHETTO VAN-GO"), Poet/Spoken Word Artist, Vocalist, AUTHOR, ACTIVIST, VEGAN VEGETARIAN and PHILOSOPHER.

AS a member of THE UNIVERSAL ZULU NATION, THE TEMPLE OF HIP HOP and AGAPE INTERNATIONAL SPIRITUAL CENTER, he seeks to use each and every element of HIP HOP to inspire, educate, motivate and redirect the inner-city youth and the HIP HOP COMMUNITIES WORLDWIDE to a place of balance, harmony, creativity, PEACE & LOVE.

He has not only worked for the OBAMA campaign (coined "The Obama Hip Hop Hype Man"), he has also been on stage and on tour with KRS-ONE, GRANDMASTER FLASH, KOOL HERC, BUSY BEE, PUBLIC ENEMY, KOOL MO DEE, GRANDMASTER CAZ, PARIS, TUPAC and ERYKAH BADU just to name a few.

HE is and will be, until he passes on to the next dimension, truly the personification of HIP HOP, Poetry, Funk & Soul music.

DIARY OF A BLACK MAN....

# DISCOGRAPHY:

| | | |
|---|---|---|
| DIARY OF A BLAKMAN. C.D. | (1998) | SPOKEN WORD |
| ESCAPE FROM L.A. C.D. | (1999) | SPOKEN WORD |
| UNPLUGGED C.D. | (2002) | SPOKEN WORD |
| (LIVE & UNCENSORED) C.D. | (2003) | SPOKEN WORD |
| P.O.E.T. | (2005) | SPOKEN WORD/HIP HOP |
| A PICTURE'S WORTH C.D. | (2006) | SPOKEN WORD |
| FREE THE JENA 6 | (2007) | HIP HOP SINGLE |
| KATRINA vs. WILLIE LYNCH | (2007) | HIP HOP SINGLE |
| I BARACK THE MIC RIGHT C.D | (2008) | HIP HOP/RAP |
| A.G.A.P.E | (2009) | HIP HOP/SOUL/GOSPEL |
| ELV8TE | (2009) | HIP HOP/HOUSE/FUNK |
| HELP HAITI | (2010) | HIP HOP SINGLE |

DIARY OF A BLACK MAN....

# BOOKS:

| | | |
|---|---|---|
| DIARY OF A BLACKMAN | (1998) | POETRY |
| BLACK HISTORY 101 | (1999) | POETRY |
| 100% NATURAL | (1999) | POETRY |
| BLACK LOVE | (1999) | POETRY |
| HUEMANITY | (1999) | POETRY |
| SPIRIT INSIDE | (2000) | POETRY |
| MASTERPIECES | (2002) | POETRY |
| A PICTURE'S WORTH... | (2006) | POETRY/ART |
| LIFE'S A BEACH (& then U die) | (2011) | Autobiography |
| * How to Vend And Win !!! | (2011) | Instructional Manual |
| * More Than Just Words... | (2011) | Acronyms |
| * (Always Resonating Truth) | (2011) | Art |
| * Do u Understand the words ? | (2011) | Quotes |

*(Still in the process of publishing)

DIARY OF A BLACK MAN....

## MERCHANDISE:

*CONSCIOUS ENTERPRISES* (1998) *Political Apparel*
*Fly Dye Art* (2002) *Visual Art/Merchandise*
*Barack Is Beautiful* (2008) *Obama Merchandise*

# For bookings, products or other info:

## CONSCIOUS ENTERPRISES/ FLY DYE ART

c/o ANTHONY BROWN (TONY B. CONSCIOUS )
PO Box 75882 la, ca 90075
Cell: (323)251-4969

EMAIL(S):  fly_dye@hotmail.com   art info
          Flydye_art@hotmail.com   Art shows
          B_conscious@hotmail.com  Music, Poetry
          Teamobama@hotmail.com  Obama/political
          Flydyeart@gmail.com   International info

* ALL E-MAIL INQUIRIES WILL BE ANSWERED PROMPTLY.

DIARY OF A BLACK MAN....

# ONLINE SITES & LINKS

## *Personal WEBSITES:*

www.tonybconscious.com

www.flydye.com

www.flydyeart.com

www.poetrygear.com

www.beautifulbarack.com

## *Social Networks / Online Stores:*

www.facebook.com/tonybconscious1

www.facebook.com/tonybconscious2

www.twitter.com/B_conscious

www.myspace.com/tonybconscious

www.myspace.com/flydye

www.youtube.com/tonybconscious

www.tunecore.com/music/tonybconscious

www.ourstage.com/fanclub/tonybconscious

www.elevatepresents.com/profile/TONYBCONSCIOUS

www.reverbnation.com/tonybconscious

www.modelrun.com/actor/tonybconscious

www.nextcat.com/tonybconscious

http://venice311.org/venice-boardwalk/boardwalk-vendors-artists-performers/venice-beach-artist-performer-activist-directory/tony-b-conscious/

## KEEP IN TOUCH !!!
# TONY B. CONSCIOUS

DIARY OF A BLACK MAN....

www.ingramcontent.com/pod-product-compliance
Lightning Source LLC
Chambersburg PA
CBHW080440110426
42743CB00016B/3229